Microsoft Dynamics GP Workflow 2.0

Second Edition

Ian Grieve

First published: March 2017

ISBN 978-0-9930556-5-2

http://publishing.azurecurve.co.uk

About the Author

Ian Grieve is a Microsoft® Most Valuable Professional for Microsoft Dynamics GP and is an Advanced Credentialed Professional in Microsoft Dynamics GP by the Association of Dynamics Professionals. He is the ERP Practice Manager at Perfect Image Ltd., a Microsoft Partner and VAR in the North East of England.

Ian has worked with Microsoft Dynamics GP since 2003 and, over the years since then, has dealt with all aspects of the product life-cycle from presales, to implementation, to technical and functional training, to post go-live support and subsequent upgrades and process reviews.

Ian is the author of *Microsoft Dynamics GP 2013 Financial Management, Microsoft Dynamics GP Workflow 2.0* and *Implementing the Microsoft Dynamics GP Web Client,* co-author of *Microsoft Dynamics GP 2013 Cookbook* and *Microsoft Dynamics GP 2016 Cookbook*, produced the *Microsoft Dynamics GP Techniques* online learning course and was the technical reviewer for several Microsoft Dynamics CRM books published by Packt Publishing.

In his spare time, Ian runs the *azurecurve | Ramblings of a Dynamics GP Consultant* (http://www.azurecurve.co.uk) blog dedicated to Microsoft Dynamics GP and related products.

Acknowledgement

Thanks to my parents for their support through the years and my employer, Perfect Image, for giving me the opportunity to work clients in many different fields and, not least, for being open to me taking on outside projects such as this book and its predecessors.

I also owe thanks to all of the clients I have worked with over the years, whose needs and questions have prompted me to learn ever more about Microsoft Dynamics GP, thereby putting me in a position to write this book.

Thanks to the Technical Reviewers, Mark Polino, fellow Microsoft® Most Valuable Professional, and my colleague Jamie Harris for their valuable feedback which helped to make the book better.

And also thanks to Andy Evans, one of my clients, for the proof-reading he did after buying the last version. His feedback is much appreciated.

About the Reviewers

Mark Polino

Mark is a CPA and Certified Information Technology Professional for Dynamics GP. He has worked with Dynamics GP since 1999 as both a consultant and a user. Currently, Mark is Director of Client Services at Fastpath, Inc. and he also runs the popular DynamicAccounting.net website dedicated to Microsoft Dynamics GP. Mark is the author or co-author of 6 books on Dynamics GP.

Jamie Harris

Jamie Harris is the Application Support Consultant Team Leader at Perfect Image Ltd., a Microsoft Partner and VAR in the North East of England. Jamie's venture into the world of ERP started in 2006 working for Sage, supporting a range of Accounts products.

In 2014 he moved to Perfect Image and was introduced to Microsoft Dynamics GP; after spending time supporting users with the product he progressed to working under Ian Grieve in the ERP Practice as an ERP Consultant, implementing and customizing the software.

Since then, he has been promoted to Application Support Consultant Team Leader and leads the team responsible for supporting new and existing implementations of Microsoft Dynamics GP.

Table of Contents

Preface

Microsoft Dynamics GP is a popular enterprise resource planning (ERP) application used by tens of thousands of sites around the world to keep the accounting, financial, distribution and manufacturing functions running day in and day out.

Dynamics GP includes a variety of tools and modules to assist in controlling processes and data; one of the major modules for this was the Dynamics Workflow module. However, this module had major flaws which very much limited its usefulness; it was slow, clunky and difficult to install, configure and maintain.

As of Microsoft Dynamics GP 2013 R2 this Workflow module has been replaced with a new one; Workflow 2.0. This new module lives entirely within Dynamics GP itself, thereby removing the dependency on SharePoint; this has the dual benefit of making Workflow 2.0 easy to setup, configure workflow processes and maintain on an ongoing basis.

The initial release of Workflow 2.0 had workflows available for approving purchase requisitions, purchase orders and timesheets for both Project and Payroll; Microsoft Dynamics GP 2015 saw the introduction of workflow for additional areas of the system such as batch approval in General Ledger, Payables Management and Receivables Management.

Microsoft Dynamics GP 2015 R2 added two additional workflow types; SmartLIst Designer Views and Payables Management Transaction approval which allows individual invoices to be submitted for approval.

The Payables Management Transaction approval workflow was the most requested workflow type on Microsoft Connect (http://connect.microsoft.com/).

Workflow 2.0 also allows actions to be performed via email without the using needing to be logged into Microsoft Dynamics GP.

Who This Book Is For

This book is aimed at Dynamics GP users, partners and consultants who intend to utilize Workflow 2.0 to gain more control of the approval process.

This book assumes you have very basic knowledge of Windows Server, Active Directory for creating users and groups and a basic knowledge of Microsoft Dynamics GP. The final chapter *Chapter 9, Installing Web Services for Microsoft Dynamics GP*, is aimed at a more technical user than the rest of the book.

What This Book Covers

This book introduces the concepts of workflow and moves onto Workflow 2.0. It covers the creation of both simple and complex document based workflow processes, a non-document based workflow, how users interact with the workflow process, including email notifications and email actions, before wrapping up with a step-by-step install and verification of the Web Services for Microsoft Dynamics GP.

How This Book Is Structured

Chapter 1, Introduction to Microsoft Dynamics Workflow 2.0, *introduces the basic concepts of workflow and then the functionality of Microsoft Dynamics GP Workflow 2.0.*

Chapter 2, Setting up Microsoft Dynamics GP Workflow 2.0, covers the setup of Workflow 2.0.

Chapter 3, Workflow Maintenance, introduces the Workflow Maintenance window and how a workflow process is created and activated.

Chapter 4, Creating a Simple Batch Approval Workflow, covers the creation of a simple General Ledger Batch Approval workflow process.

Chapter 5, Interacting with the workflow process, covers the ways of interacting with the workflow process including E-mail for Workflow and E-mail Actions.

Chapter 6, Creating a Complex Purchase Requisition Workflow, covers the creation of a complex purchase requisition workflow process.

Chapter 7, Creating a Vendor Approval Workflow, covers the creation of a vendor approval workflow.

Chapter 8, Adding Additional Tables for Workflow Conditions, covers the creation of new table relationships to extend the available workflow conditions.

Chapter 9, Installing Web Services for Microsoft Dynamics GP, covers the installation, configuration and verification of the Web Services for Microsoft Dynamics GP which are required if E-mail Actions are going to be used.

What You Need For This Book

You will require the following for this book:

- One Windows Server 2012 R2 with a domain controller.

- One Windows Server 2012 R2 with Microsoft SQL Server 2014 (this could be the same server as the first).

- One Windows Server 2012 R2 with Exchange 2013 or other mail server; on a test deployment I typically use hMailServer as it is lighter and easier to configure.

- One, or more, servers with Windows Server 2012 R2 with Microsoft Dynamics GP 2016 (again this could be the same server as the first).

- The Fabrikam, Inc. sample company deployed.

Windows Server 2012 and SQL Server 2012 are acceptable replacements for Windows Server 2012 R2 and SQL Server 2014 listed above as both are fully compatible with Microsoft Dynamics GP 2016.

I would recommend using the above setup as a trial run before trying to implement Microsoft Dynamics GP Workflow 2.0 on a live system if you plan to use email actions which have a requirement for the Web Services for Microsoft Dynamics GP; on a test system a copy of the live system can be used in place of the Fabrikam, Inc. sample company.

For a test system, all of the above could be located on a single server although I typically keep the domain controller separate.

Conventions

To help you get the most from this book and keep track of what is happening, a number of stylistic conventions have been used throughout this book.

The key styles of text used in this book to distinguish between different types of information are:

- New terms and important words are **bolded**.

- Words you would type are shown as AZURECURVE\srvc.webservices.

- Key combinations are shown as *Win+R*.

Errata

Every care has been taken to ensure the accuracy of the books content, but mistakes do happen. If you find a mistake in this book we would be grateful if you could report this to us; reporting an error means we can fix the error and improve future editions of the book.

Please report errors by visiting http://publishing.azurecurve.co.uk/submit-errata, select the book in question from the drop down list and enter the details of the errata in the textbox.

Reader Feedback

Feedback from readers is always welcomed as it will enable us to improve future titles.

Please let us know what you think about this book, in particular what you liked and disliked.

If you are having problems with any aspect of the book, or have questions about the content you can contact us at questions.book@azurecurve.co.uk.

Piracy

The Internet is a marvelous invention, but it does represent an ongoing problem for the protection of published works. If you happen across any unlicensed copies of our works, in any form, please provide us with the website name or link, so that we can pursue a remedy, by email at copyright@azurecurve.co.uk.

1

Introduction to Microsoft Dynamics GP Workflow 2.0

Microsoft Dynamics GP has long had a Workflow module available, but it was one which required SharePoint and was not very user friendly to use, and was what I would almost go so far as to describe as verging on the hostile to the person trying to install and configure it. As of Microsoft Dynamics GP 2013 a new Workflow module, known as Workflow 2.0, was introduced. This module is a core part of Microsoft Dynamics GP and is both easy to setup and use.

What is workflow?

Before we get started introducing Dynamics GP Workflow 2.0, it might be useful to introduce the basic concepts of workflow in general. At its simplest level, the term **workflow** refers to the automating of the steps of a business process.

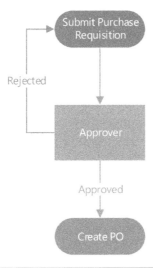

For example, when a buyer raises a purchase order, the workflow process replaces the traditional method of communicating the purchase order to the budget holder through a memo, phone call or email by sending a message to the correct budget holder to approve the purchase order.

A workflow process will generally be more complicated than the example given above in that it can require not only approval by one or more people, but also that several steps be undertaken before the approval step.

Introducing Workflow 2.0

Workflow 2.0 replaces the old Dynamics Workflow module which had prerequisites of SharePoint and Web Services for Microsoft Dynamics GP. The new workflow module does not use SharePoint at all and, while it still uses Web Services, the use of Web Services is only required for the more advanced email actions feature of Workflow 2.0.

Since its introduction, Workflow 2.0 has been well received by the Dynamics GP Community due to its ease of configuration and use.

Microsoft Dynamics GP 2013 R2 was the first version to include the new Workflow 2.0 functionality, but this version was fairly restricted in the number of workflows and only included the following:

1. Purchase Requisition Approval.

2. Purchase Order Approval.

3. Payroll Timecard Approval.

4. Project PTE Timesheet Approval.

Microsoft Dynamics GP 2015 saw the introduction of nine new workflow types:

1. General Ledger Batch Approval.

2. Vendor Approval.

3. Payables Batch Approval.

4. Receivables Batch Approval.

5. Project PTE Expense Approval.

6. Employee Profile Approval.

7. Employee Skills and Training Approval.

8. Direct Deposit Approval.

9. W4 Approval.

Microsoft Dynamics GP 2015 R2 contained two new workflow types:

1. Payables Invoice Approval workflow type which allows individual invoices to be sent for approval. This is an example of Microsoft listening to the community as this was the most requested new workflow type on the Microsoft Connect website (http://connect.microsoft.com/).

2. SmartList Designer View Approval workflow type which allows a view to be created in SmartList Designer and submitted for approval.

Workflow 2.0 Prerequisites

The prerequisites for the core functionality of Workflow 2.0 are fairly simple. To use the core Workflow 2.0 functionality you need a working implementation of Microsoft Dynamics GP on an Active Directory domain (which is also a requirement for the Dynamics GP Web Client and Management Reporter).

If you want to send notification emails then an SMTP server is required to send the email. This can, but does not need to, be Microsoft Exchange; for the writing of this book I configured and used hMailServer. To follow the examples you will need the connection details for an SMTP server.

I've heard a number of people stating that Workflow 2.0 requires an Microsoft Exchange server for sending emails, but this is not correct. Any SMTP server can be used.

For email notifications to work, all users will need an email address defined against them in Active Directory; the emails are sent to users based on an AD lookup so any user in AD who does not have an email address assigned will not receive an email. However, it should be noted that no error will be raised should the lookup fail.

Should you want to use email actions, then the prerequisites are somewhat more complicated as, in addition to the above, the Web Services for Microsoft Dynamics GP are also required.

The SMTP server sends the email from Workflow 2.0 and the Web Services for Microsoft Dynamics GP are used to present the interactive form to the user where they can either approve, reject or delegate the document. In *Chapter 9, Installing Web Services for Microsoft Dynamics GP* we'll be covering the installation, configuration and verification of the Web Services.

Workflow 2.0 Windows

There are only four windows accessible from the menu used to setup and maintain Workflow 2.0. The windows are all accessible from the Setup menu in the Administration series:

1. Workflow Setup allows both email and email actions to be enabled and configured. This window is only needed if emails will be used with Workflow; if all approvals are done by users who usually access the Microsoft Dynamics GP client, either desktop or web, then email and email actions do not need to be used.

   This window is on the System menu, but is actually a company one; if you intend to use email notifications in a company, you will need to configure this window in each company.

2. Workflow Maintenance is a company setup window where the workflow processes are created and maintained.

3. Workflow Calendar is a company setup window where working days and times can be defined.

4. E-mail Message Setup allows the creation of the messages which will be emailed to the user for notification or approval (or rejection).

Workflow 2.0 Email Notifications

Workflow 2.0 can be configured to send an email notification to a user in two types of circumstances. Firstly, it can be configured to send an email to the originator as the document progresses through the workflow process. Secondly, it can be configured to send an email to users when they are assigned a task or approval to perform.

Email Notifications are very useful when approvers are not usually logged into Microsoft Dynamics GP regularly. If they are a regular user then they can see notifications on their homepage or via one of the navigation lists.

Workflow 2.0 Email Actions

Email Actions are an optional component of Workflow 2.0 which provide users the ability to interact with submitted batches or items without the need to log into Microsoft Dynamics GP. Instead the user can click a link within the email notification which launches a window displaying details of the approval step which they can interact with by clicking to approve or reject.

Why Use Email Actions?

The main reason for using Email Actions is that it allows users who are not typically Microsoft Dynamics GP users to approve documents without needing to log into Microsoft Dynamics GP.

Instead users can simply click the link on the email and perform the approval, rejection or delegation via the resulting web page which is displayed by the Web Services for Microsoft Dynamics GP.

The additional benefit of the user not logging into Microsoft Dynamics GP is that a license is not required.

Workflow 2.0 on the Home screen

The Microsoft Dynamics GP home screen was also updated in Microsoft Dynamics GP 2013 to have workflow related sections which could be added. These sections both display information on the documents to be viewed and also allows windows or navigation lists to be loaded.

Navigation Panes

A number of new navigation lists were introduced alongside Workflow 2.0. These preconfigured lists present the documents at the different stages of the workflow process (typically Saved and Not Approved); each navigation list has an action pane which allows interaction with the submitted documents to submit, approve, reject and so on.

Summary

In this chapter we have introduced the basic concepts of workflow and the new Workflow 2.0 which was introduced in Microsoft Dynamics GP 2013 R2. In the next chapter we will cover the setup of Workflow 2.0.

2

Setting up
Microsoft Dynamics GP
Workflow 2.0

In this chapter we're going to take a look at the steps required to set up Workflow 2.0. The setup covered is the setup of Workflow 2.0 within Microsoft Dynamics GP; the installation of Microsoft Dynamics GP itself or installation of email is not within the scope of this chapter.

Workflow Setup

The Workflow Setup window is accessible through the Administration series, under Setup >> System. This is the window where the E-mail for Workflow and E-mail Actions can be enabled and configured should you want to use email notifications or email actions.

Workflow 2.0 is fully functional even if you choose not to use either the email notifications or email actions; however, if you don't use them then you will be missing a large chunk of very useful functionality.

E-Mail for Workflow

E-mail for Workflow provides notifications to users; these notifications can be to the user who has submitted the workflow when it passes through different stages, such as submission, rejection, approval, delegation and so on.

To enable E-Mail for Workflow, perform the following steps:

1. Open **Workflow Setup** window from the **Administration** series and clicking on **Workflow Setup** under **Setup >> Company >> Workflow**.

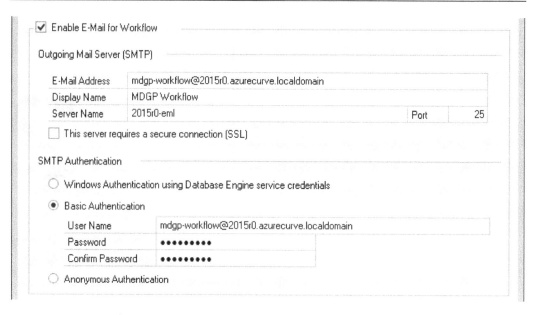

2. Mark the **Enable E-Mail for Workflow** checkbox.

3. Under the **Outgoing Mail Server (SMTP)** label:

   a. Enter the **E-Mail Address** from which Workflow emails should be sent.

   b. Enter the **Display Name** which is the friendly name which is included on the email.

   c. Enter the SMTP server name or IP address in the **Server Name** field.

   d. Enter the port the SMTP server is listening on in the **Port** field; the default SMTP port is 25, but this will depend on the options chosen when installing the SMTP server.

4. Under the **SMTP Authentication** label, choose the authentication method that will be used to authenticate with the SMTP server; the setting you choose here will depend on the configuration of the SMTP server being used. If you opt for **Basic Authentication** you will need to enter the following fields:

   a. **User Name**.

   b. **Password**

   c. **Confirm Password**.

Once these settings have been entered, there is a facility available to test that they are correct and working. To test them perform the following steps:

1. Click the **Test E-Mail** button on the action pane.

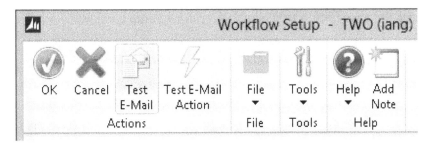

2. This will open the **Test Workflow E-Mail** window; enter your email address in the **To** field.

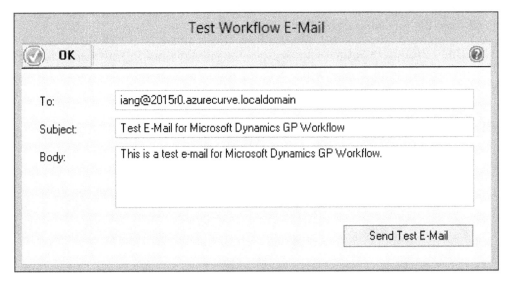

3. If desired, the **Subject** or **Body** may be amended, then click the **Send Test E-Mail** button in the bottom right corner of the window.

4. Once the email has been sent a dialog will be displayed with a message to check your mailbox to make sure the email was received (if you don't see the email it is worth checking the spam folder). Click **OK** to dismiss the dialog.

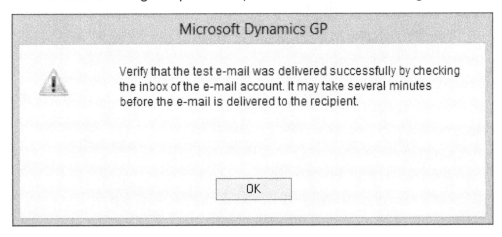

5. Click the **Save** button to close the **Workflow Setup** window.

Office 365 Integration with E-Mail for Workflow

Office 365 is becoming a more popular option for companies using Microsoft Dynamics GP and can be used with Workflow 2.0. the setup is not any more complicated than that required for an on premise Exchange, or other email, server once you have the connection details for the Office 365 SMTP server.

If you are using **Office 365 for Business** the SMTP server is **smtp.office365.com**, the port is **587** and you will need to enable **SSL**. To configure **E-Mail for Workflow** to use Office 365, perform the following steps:

1. Open **Workflow Setup** window from the **Administration** series and clicking on **Workflow Setup** under **Setup >> Company >> Workflow**.

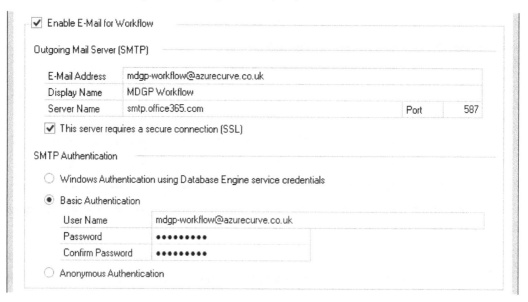

2. Mark the **Enable E-Mail for Workflow** checkbox.

3. Under the **Outgoing Mail Server (SMTP)** label:

   a. Enter the **E-Mail Address** from which Workflow emails should be sent.

   b. Enter the **Display Name** which is the friendly name which is included on the email.

   c. Enter smtp.office365.com in the **Server Name** field.

   d. Enter 587 in the **Port** field.

   e. Mark the **This server requires a secure connection (SSL)**.

4. Under the **SMTP Authentication** label, choose the authentication method that

will be used to authenticate with the SMTP server; the setting you choose here will depend on the configuration of the SMTP server being used. If you opt for **Basic Authentication** you will need to enter the following fields:

    a.   **User Name**.

    b.   **Password**

    c.   **Confirm Password**.

If you are not using **Office 365 for Business**, but are using an Exchange-based email you can look up your settings by performing the following steps:

1. Sign in to **Outlook Web App**.

2. On the nav bar, either choose **Outlook** (or **Mail**), or choose **App launcher >> Outlook**.

3. On the nav bar, click **Settings >> Options**.

4. Under **Options**, click **Account >> My account**.

5. On the **My account** page, select **Settings for POP or IMAP access** or under **Mail > Accounts**, select **POP and IMAP**.

6. The **SMTP** server name, port and SSL/TLS requirements listed on the **Settings for POP or IMAP Access** page under **SMTP setting**.

Once you have the settings you can enter them in the **Workflow Setup** window.

E-Mail Actions

An email action is what allows the user to approve, reject or delegate a document without being logged into Microsoft Dynamics GP.

Before **E-Mail Actions** can be enabled, Web Services for Microsoft Dynamics GP needs to be installed. This is covered in *Chapter 9, Installing Web Services for Microsoft Dynamics GP*.

To enable **E-Mail Actions**, perform the following steps:

1. Open the **Workflow Setup** window from the **Administration** series and clicking on **Workflow Setup** under **Setup >> Company >> Workflow**.

2. Mark the **Enable E-Mail Actions** checkbox.

3. Enter the **Server Name** of the server which has the Web Services installed.

4. The **Port** field will display the Dynamics GP Web Services default port; change this if required.

5. If the Dynamics GP Web Services installation binding has been configured with an SSL certificate, then mark the **This server requires a secure connection (SSL)** checkbox.

As with the **E-Mail for Workflow**, there is a facility to test that the **E-Mail Actions** can communicate with the web services successfully. Do this by performing the following steps:

1. Click the **Test E-Mail Action** button on the action pane.

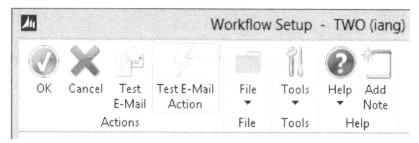

2. A dialog will be displayed confirming the test was successful. Click **OK** to dismiss the dialog.

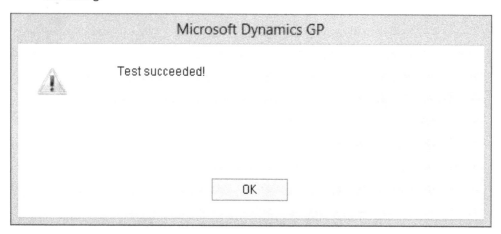

3. Click **Save** to close the **Workflow Setup** window.

Workflow Calendar

The next step in configuring Workflow 2.0 is to configure the **Workflow Calendar**; this calendar is used to define both working days and working hours. The calendar is used by Workflow 2.0 when calculating time spans in order to determine when a task or approval step is due or overdue.

To configure the **Workflow Calendar**, perform the following steps:

1. Open the **Workflow Setup** window from the **Administration** series and clicking on **Workflow Setup** under **Setup >> Company >> Workflow**.

2. The window is split into two sections. The first is the **Work Days** which has a default of Monday to Friday and the hours of 0800 to 1700 for each day. To change these mark or unmark the checkboxes next to each day and type the times into the **Start Time** and **End Time** fields.

3. The second section of the window allows the **Non-work Days** to be configured. To configure the non-working days:

    a. Select the **Year**.

    b. Enter the **Date** for the first non-working day.

    c. Enter a **Description** that describes why the date has been entered.

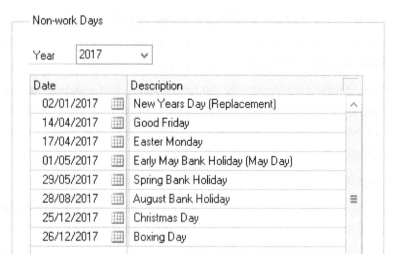

d. Repeat for all non-working days that year; the example above shows the UK Bank Holidays for 2017.

4. Click the **Save** button on the action pane to save the changes and close the **Workflow Calendar**.

As an example, if a Workflow Calendar is defined with working days starting at 0900 and ending at 1730, with Saturdays and Sundays and the UK Bank Holidays entered above as non-working days, then a document submitted at 1700 on Friday 22nd December, assuming an 8 hour time limit, would become overdue if not approved by 1000 on Wednesday 28th December due to the weekend and Christmas Day and Boxing Day Bank Holidays.

Workflow E-mail Message Setup

The **Workflow E-Mail Message Setup** window allows the email subject and body of the **Workflow Assignment** and **Workflow Action Completed** emails to be defined. This window works the same as the **Message Setup** window used to configure the **Subject** and **Body** for the emails which accompany the **Word Templates**.

While the default messages are fairly useful, they can be made much more so by including some of the detail from the transaction. Including more detail about the transaction, such as the lines of a purchase requisition, should be done so that the approver has all required information available to them before approving using one of the email actions.

To amend one of the email messages to add the detail lines, perform the following steps:

1. Open the **Message Setup** window by clicking **E-mail Message Setup** from the **Administration menu** under **Setup** and **Company**.

2. Enter a **Message ID** or click the lookup button and locate the one to edit.

3. In the **Body** section of the window, add a couple of blank lines below the **Document Amount**.

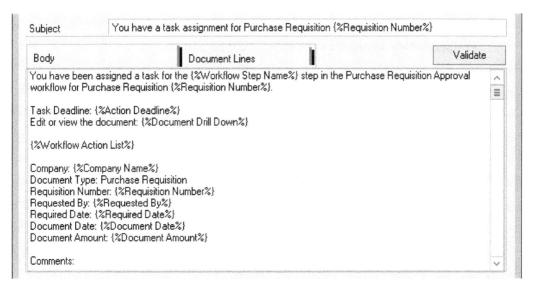

4. In **Select and Insert Fields** click the **Field** dropdown list and select **Document Line Fields**.

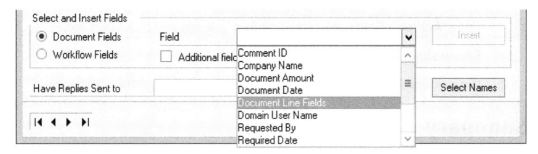

5. Click **Insert** to insert the selected item to the **Body** field.

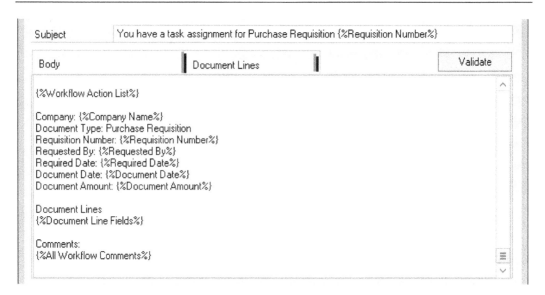

6. With the **Document Line Fields** added to the body of the email, the next step is to select which document line fields should be output.

   Click the **Document Lines** tab.

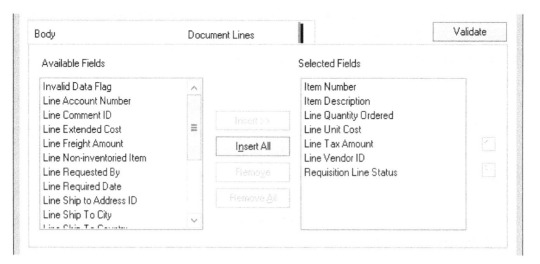

7. Under **Available Fields**, select the first field to insert and click **Insert >>**.

8. Repeat step 7 for each required field.

9. Once all fields have been selected, click the **Save** button on the action pane.

Summary

In this chapter we have covered the setup of Workflow 2.0 by configuring the **E-Mail for Workflow**, **E-Mail Actions**, **Workflow Calendar** and **Workflow E-Mail Messages**. In the next chapter we're going to take a look at the **Workflow Maintenance** window.

3

Introducing the Workflow Maintenance window

The Workflow Maintenance window, accessible though the Company Setup menu in the Administration series, is where workflow processes are created and maintained. The Workflow Maintenance window contains a number of different elements which this chapter will explain in detail. Then, in *Chapter 4*, *Creating a Simple Batch Approval Workflow*, we'll move onto creating the first workflow process.

Workflow Maintenance window layout

The **Workflow Maintenance** window is the window where all workflow processes are created and maintained.

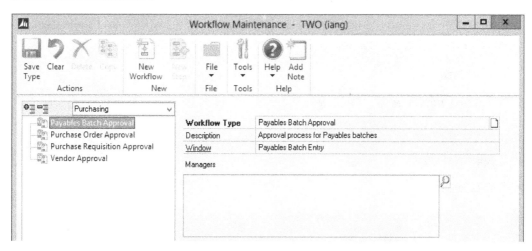

The window has three main components:

1. The action pane at the top of the window which has six buttons which are applicable to workflow:

    a. **Save** which changes depending on what is loaded; **Save Type**, **Save**

Workflow or **Save Workflow Step**.

b. **Clear** which discards any changes.

c. **Delete** which is available only for workflows and workflow steps; you cannot delete a workflow type.

d. **Copy** which allows a workflow process to be duplicated; the button is disabled unless a workflow is loaded. The copy function allows companies to be copied both within the same company and also between company databases.

e. **New Workflow** which is enabled only when a workflow step is not loaded.

f. **New Step** which is enabled only when a workflow or workflow step is loaded.

2. The navigation pane containing the tree view of workflow types and the workflows they contain which is located at the left side of the window. The navigation pane only shows the workflow types for the module selected in the drop down list above the tree view.

3. Detail pane which occupies the majority of the window and which changes layout to match the item selected in the navigation pane.

Navigation Pane Icons

The navigation pane on the left of the window displays all workflows and their steps; all nodes in the tree are accompanied by one of the icons shown below:

⬚   Workflow type

⬚   Inactive workflow

⊘   Active workflow

☑   Approval step

⬚   Task step

⚠   Unsaved workflow or workflow step

These icons can make working with workflows easier; in particular the one signifying which workflow is active as it is very easy to create a workflow, but then miss the step required to activate the workflow. When creating a workflow keep your eyes open for the green check as it's absence signifies that the workflow has not been made active.

Workflow Type

Each workflow created is created with a workflow type which defines the purpose of the workflow. When a workflow type is selected there are four fields displayed in the detail pane:

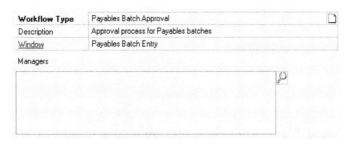

1. **Workflow Type** – confirms the selected workflow type.

2. **Description** – displays a description of the selected workflow type.

3. **Window** – displays the window associated with the workflow type and is accompanied by a link to the relevant window; in the example, above, the link is to **Payables Batch Entry**.

4. **Managers** – displays the selected managers for the workflow type. A manager is able to create and maintain this type of workflow; at least one manager is required before a workflow can be activated.

Maintaining Managers

Managers are maintained via the **Managers** field when a workflow type has been selected. Typically the managers defined against a workflow type will be either members of the IT team or super-users rather than an ordinary user of Microsoft Dynamics GP.

To add managers for a workflow type, perform the following steps:

1. Open **Workflow Maintenance** window from the **Administration** series and clicking on **Workflow Setup** under **Setup >> Company >> Workflow**.

2. Select a **Series**.

3. Select a **Workflow Type**.

4. Click the lookup button next to the **Managers** field to open the **Workflow User Selection** window.

5. In the **Find** field, type the name of the user you want to add as a manager and click the binoculars button. A lookup will be performed on Active Directory; if successful the user's AD user name will be displayed.

6. Click **Add** to add them to the **Selected Users** list.

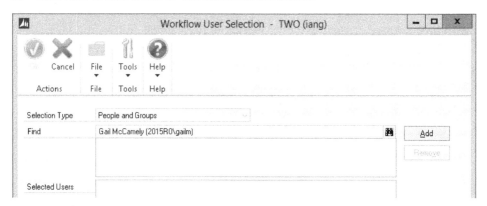

7. Repeat steps 5 and 6 for each user you want to add as a manager for the workflow type.

8. Click **OK** to close the **Workflow User Selection** window.

To remove managers for a workflow type, perform the following steps:

1. Open **Workflow Maintenance** window from the **Administration** series and clicking on **Workflow Setup** under **Setup >> Company >> Workflow**.

2. Select a **Series**.

3. Select a **Workflow Type**.

4. Click the lookup button next to the **Managers** field to open the **Workflow User Selection** window.

5. Select the user in the **Selected Users** list.

6. Click the **Remove** button.

7. Repeat steps 5 and 6 for each user you want to remove as a manager for the workflow type.

8. Click **OK** to close the **Workflow User Selection** window.

Workflow Process

The workflow process contains the options and rules for how an overdue task is handled as well as the steps.

Creating the Workflow Process

To create a new workflow process, perform the following steps:

1. Click the **New Workflow** button on the action pane.

New
Workflow

This will cause the detail pane to change to show the workflow creation layout.

Workflow Name	New Workflow		☐ Active
Description			
Workflow Type	General Ledger Batch Approval		

Step	Condition	Assignment

Options:

- ☐ Send notifications for completed actions
- ☐ Allow approver to delegate tasks
- ☐ Allow originator to be an approver
- ☐ Always require at least one approver
- ☐ Use alternate final approver

When a task is overdue:

- ● Take no action
- ○ Escalate to next approver
- ○ Escalate to:
- ○ Automatically reject the overdue task

2. Enter the name of the new **Workflow Name** field.

3. Enter a **Description**, which can be longer and more detailed than the name.

4. Several settings are available in the options pane:

   a. **Send notifications for completed actions** can be marked to send email notifications to users.

   b. The blue expansion arrow opens the **Workflow Email Notification Maintenance** window where the different types of notifications can be enabled and the message selected.

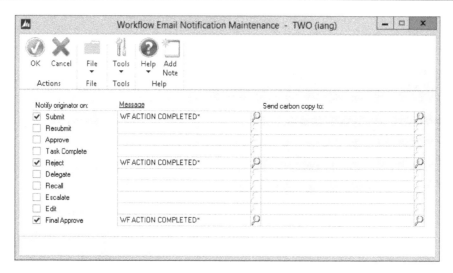

c. Marking **Allow approver to delegate tasks** allows an approver to delegate the approval to another user.

d. Mark **Allow originator to be an approver** to allow the user who submitted the batch to also approve it; in most circumstances you would not want this checkbox to be marked to maintain a separation of duties.

e. Mark **Always require at least one approver** to enforce approval by at least one person.

f. Marking **Use alternative final approver** allows a user to be selected to be the final approver. The alternate approver is assigned to the approval action under the following conditions:

    i. The Always Require at Least One Approver option is marked and there are no approval steps whose conditions are met.

    ii. The Always Require at Least One Approver option is marked and the approver edits the document and there are no following approval steps.

    iii. There are no approval steps following an overdue step, depending on your escalation settings.

5. Determine the action required when a task is overdue. There are four options available:

a. **Take No action**.

b. **Escalate to next approver.**

c. **If you mark Escalate to** a user must then be selected; this user is the user to whom the task will be escalated.

     d. **Automatically reject the overdue task**.

6. Click the **Save Workflow** button.

Creating a Workflow Step

A workflow process can contain either one or many workflow steps with the user defining the order in which they are processed.

Additionally, the conditions for running the step, the users the step is assigned to and also the completion policy for the step can be defined.

One key point to remember when dealing with Workflow 2.0 is that it is an *approval* process. Every step is an approval step, so you can't have a step which is just a conditional step.

For example, assume a purchase requisition workflow where following rules were to be checked:

1. If Buyer = Laura Bowie and the Subtotal < 500 send to Ian Grieve for approval.

2. If Buyer = Laura Bowie and the Subtotal is between 500 and 2000 then send to Bob Oliver for approval.

3. If Buyer = Laura Bowie and the Subtotal > 2000 then send to William Morris for approval.

People new to Microsoft Dynamics GP Workflow 2.0 often assume that they can create a conditional step where Buyer = Laura Bowie and then have the three value checks as child steps.

However, Workflow 2.0 does not allow this type of conditional step, if you tried to configure a workflow process in this way then someone would need to approve Laura Bowie as the buyer before the approval of the value.

Instead what needs to be configured in the workflow, is all three of the above rules created as first step.

It is also important to remember that anything not falling within one of the configured steps will not bypass the workflow; instead it will be sent to the Workflow Managers for approval.

Before a step can be created, the workflow process itself needs to have been created and saved. After this, a workflow step can be created by performing the following steps:

1. Click the **New Step** button on the action pane to create a new step.

2. The detail pane will change to display the **Workflow Step** layout.

3. Enter a name in the **Step Name** field.

4. Enter a longer, more detailed **Description** for the step.

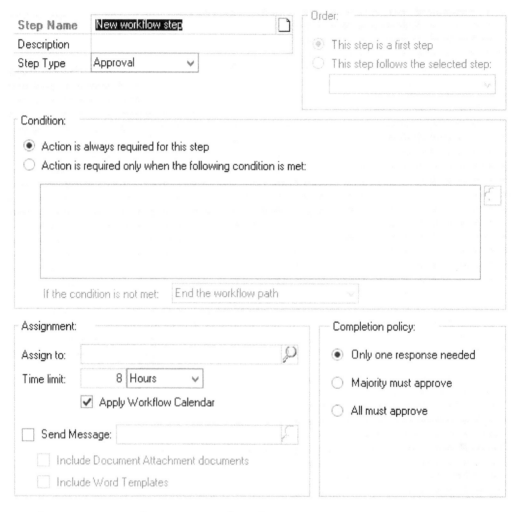

5. The **Step Type** can be set to one of the following:

   a. **Approval** which is a step allowing the user to either approve or reject the submitted item.

   b. **Task** which requires an action other an approval/rejection to be performed. This might be an action such as selecting a vendor for a purchase requisition.

6. The **Order** fields in the top right are disabled until the second workflow step is

created:

    a. At this point the first step created will have the **This step is a first step** radio button will be selected.

    b. When creating subsequent steps, the **This step follows the selected step** should be selected and a field selected in from the drop down list.

       The default Order is to have a parent of the step which was active when the New Step button was pressed

7. The **Condition** section allows when an action is required to be determined by selecting one of two options:

    a. **Action is always required for this step**.

    b. **Action is required only when the following condition is met** then enables the blue expansion arrow which opens the **Workflow Condition Editor** which allows a rule to be composed.

       i. After entering the rule, click **Add**.

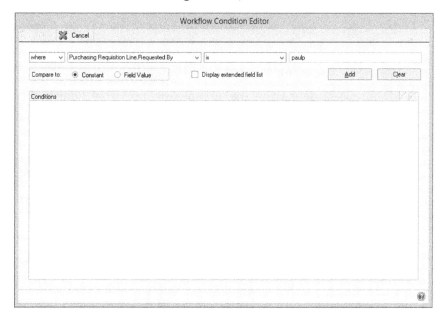

       ii. Rules can be multilevel. Once finished click the **OK** button to close the **Workflow Condition Editor** window.

    c. **If the condition is not met** allows control over what the workflow process should do when the condition being checked is not met.

       i. **End the workflow path** means the workflow will not run the subsequent steps. If there are no parallel steps which run for the workflow path, the workflow is completed and a "No Action Needed" history entry is created.

ii. **Continue to the next step** means the workflow continues to any sequential steps following the stop for which the condition was not met. The step status for the instance of the step is set to "No Action Needed".

iii. **Reject the workflow** will pending workflow user activity for all steps (approval and task) are cancelled and the status of the document is set to "Rejected".

8. In the **Assignment** section there are several fields to complete:

a. **Assign To** allows the person, or people, responsible for the step to be assigned. Assign users by clicking the lookup button which opens the **Workflow User Selection** window.

This window operates in the same way as the manager selection one; when finished click the **OK** button.

If there is only one approver, then that person is responsible for approving all documents being processed by the step.

If there are multiple approvers, the number of them which have to approve is defined in the **Completion policy** section; see below for details.

b. **Time limit** allows the length of time available to the approver to complete the step to be defined. This can be in hours, days or weeks and is used to calculate the due date of the step.

If an approver fails to respond by the due date, the task is considered overdue and will be handled according to the option selected in the **When a step is overdue** area of the Workflow Process configuration.

The time limit can only be in whole units. This may cause issues for some companies which, like Perfect Image have 7.5 hour long days; we would have to decide to go for 7 or 8 hour time limits.

c. Mark the **Apply Workflow Calendar** checkbox is use the workflow calendar to calculate the due date; the only time I would not mark this box is if I was dealing with a time limit of **Weeks**.

d. Mark the **Send Message** box and select a Message ID if a message is to be sent to the user assigned the task.

e. Mark the **Include Document Attachment documents** checkbox to allow attachments from the submitted records to be included on the email notification. This is useful for including documents such as quotations when a purchase requisition or purchase order is submitted for approval.

f. Mark the **Include Word Templates** box to have the Edit List or Posting Journal reports included on the notification email; this option is only available for General Ledger Batch Approval, Payables Batch Approval and Receivables Batch Approval.

Two pieces of configuration are required in the Template Configuration window (accessible via the Administration area page under Reports).

The first is to mark the Enable Report Templates if it is not already marked. This is the option which enables Word Templates themselves.

The second, for each company, is to mark the Edit Lists under Financial and the Posting Journals under Purchasing and Sales.

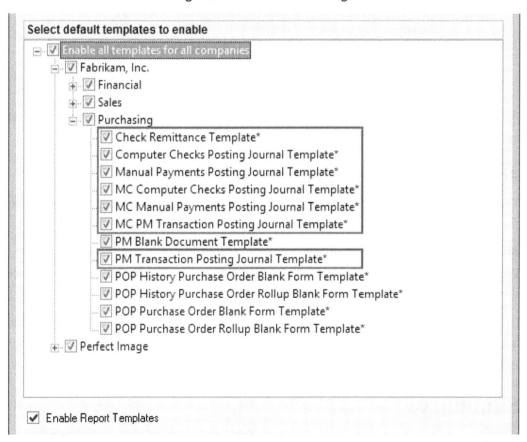

9. The **Completion policy** can be set to one of the following:

a. **Only one response needed** which, if selected, allows the action applied to be determined by the first person who responds.

If the assigned action is an **Approval**, then a single approval or rejection will allow the step to be marked as complete in the workflow.

If it is a **Task**, then only one response will allow the step to be marked as complete in the workflow.

b.   **Majority must approve** requires more than half of the assigned users to approve or complete the task depending on the type.

If there are three users, then two would need to approve/mark as complete; if there were eight assigned users then five would need to approve/mark as complete.

If the step is an approval step, then only one user clicking **Reject** is sufficient for the step be marked as rejected.

c.   **All must approve** means that all assigned users must approve the document or take the action to allow the workflow to proceed to the next step.

If only one assigned user rejects the document, it will be rejected.

10. Click the **Save Step** button on the action pane.

As many steps as required can be created to pass the document through the required approvals or actions.

Activating and Deactivating a Workflow Process

The final step in creating a workflow process is to activate it; a step which is also surprisingly easy to miss.

After configuring the workflow process and adding the required steps, select the **Workflow** in the navigation pane and mark the **Action** checkbox in the top right corner and then click the **Save Workflow** button.

Only one Workflow of each Workflow Type can be active at any one time; before making a new workflow active, the current one will need to be made inactive by unmarking the **Action** checkbox and the Save Workflow button on the action pane pressed.

Summary

In this chapter we have covered the layout of the Workflow Maintenance window and also how a workflow and its steps are created. In the next chapter, we'll take a look at creating a simple General Ledger Batch Approval Workflow.

4

Creating a Simple
Batch Approval Workflow

In the previous chapter we took a look at the Workflow Maintenance window; in this chapter we will continue to work with this window to create a simple General Ledger Batch Approval workflow.

Assigning the managers

Each type of workflow requires at least one manager to be added. So before we can create our **General Ledger Batch Approval** workflow, we need to assign one, or more, managers. To assign managers, perform the following steps:

1. Open the Workflow Maintenance window by clicking Workflow Maintenance from the **Administration menu** under Setup and Company.

2. Select Financial in the series dropdown list; with only one workflow type available under Financial, the General Ledger Batch Approval will be automatically selected and displayed in the detail pane.

3. Click the lookup button next to the multiline **Managers** field to open the **Workflow User Selection** window.

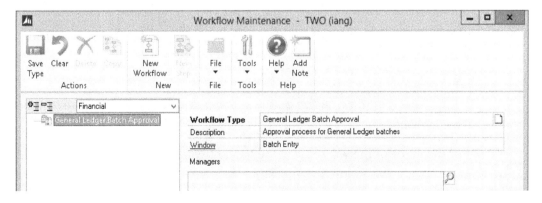

4. Type the name of the first manager and click the lookup button; this will perform a lookup on Active Directory and pull back the details of the related username.

    If there was more than one username returned, click on the user you want.

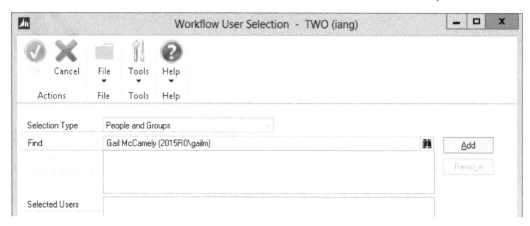

5. Click the **Add** button to add the user to the **Selected Users list**.

6. Repeat steps 2 through 4 to add any required additional managers.

7. Click the **OK** button to save the changes and close the **Workflow User Selection** window.

8. Click the **Save Type** button on the action pane to save the changes to the managers.

Creating the workflow

The workflow process we're going to create in this chapter is a very simple one-step approval process, but no matter how simple or complex the workflow is, the steps to create it are the same.

To create a workflow process, perform the following steps:

1. Open the Workflow Maintenance window by clicking Workflow Maintenance from the **Administration menu** under **Setup** and **Company**.

2. Select **Financial** in the series dropdown list; with only one workflow type available under **Financial**, the **General Ledger Batch Approval** will be automatically selected and displayed in the detail pane.

3. Click the **New Workflow** button on the action pane; this will change the content of the detail pane to show the Workflow layout.

4. Enter the name of the workflow in the **Workflow Name** field. I have entered GL Batch Approval v001; I typically enter a version number in the **Workflow**

Name to allow me to keep track of versions as they are created.

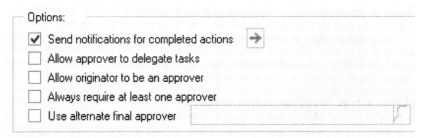

5. The **Description** field can contain a longer description of the intent of the workflow process.

6. Before creating the steps I typically configure the main options for the workflow process. If you have configured **E-mail for Workflow**, see *Chapter 2, Setting up Microsoft Dynamics GP Workflow 2.0*, mark the **Send notifications for completed actions**.

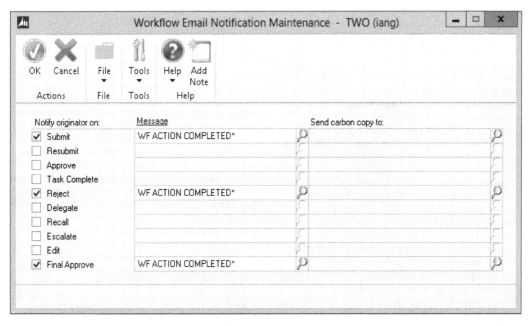

7. Click the blue expansion arrow button to open the **Workflow Email Notification Maintenance** window.

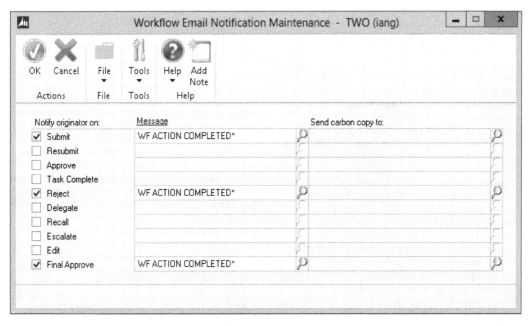

8. Mark the **Submit**, **Reject** and **Final Approve** checkboxes; if only one **Message ID** for each type of action exists, this will be defaulted into the **Message** field, otherwise you will need to click the lookup button and select the required

Message ID.

9. Click **OK** to close the **Workflow Email Notification Maintenance** window.

10. Mark the **Allow approver to delegate tasks** checkbox to allow the approver to send tasks to other people to complete.

11. Mark the **Always require at least one approver**.

12. Click the **Save Workflow** button on the action pane to save the newly created workflow process; you need to do this before any **Workflow Steps** can be created.

Creating the approval step

This first workflow process is only going to have one step as I am starting with a simple General Ledger Batch Approval workflow, but the process for creating additional steps is merely a variation on the theme. To create a workflow step, perform the following actions:

1. Click the **New Step** button on the action pane.

2. Enter Approval in the **Step Name** field.

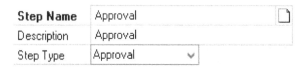

3. Enter Approval in the **Description** field; I would typically enter a longer more meaningful description in this field, but this workflow process is a simple single step one.

4. In the **Step Type**, select **Approval**.

5. Leave the **Condition** set to **Action is always required for this step**.

6. In the **Assignment** section, click the lookup button next to the **Assign to** field to open the **Workflow User Selection** window.

7. Type the user to assign the workflow to in the **Find** field and then click the lookup button to search Active Directory.

8. When the required user is returned, click the **Add** button to add the selected user to the **Selected Users** list.

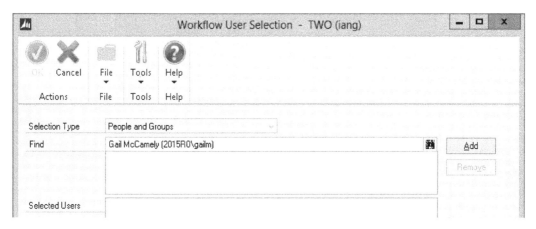

9. Click **OK** to save the selected users and close the **Workflow User Selection** window.

10. Click **Save Step** to save the step.

Activating the workflow process

Now that the workflow process and one approval step have been created, we need to activate the workflow process. To do this, perform the following steps:

1. Open the Workflow Maintenance window by clicking Workflow Maintenance from the **Administration menu** under **Setup** and **Company**.

2. Select **Financial** in the series dropdown list; with only one workflow type available under **Financial**, the **General Ledger Batch Approval** will be automatically selected and displayed in the detail pane.

3. Click on your workflow process in the list on the left of the window; in my case it is called GL Batch Approval v001.

4. Mark the **Active** checkbox in the top right of the window next to the **Workflow Name** field.

5. Click the **Save Workflow** button on the action pane.

6. Close the **Workflow Maintenance** window.

Summary

In this chapter we took a look at creating a simple General Ledger Batch Approval workflow process. In the next chapter, we will take a look at how users interact with the workflow process.

5

Interacting with a workflow process

In the previous chapter, we took a look at creating a very simple one step approval workflow process for General Ledger Batches. In this chapter we'll take a look at how the users will interact with this workflow process when creating and posting General Ledger Batches.

Submitting a document

The user would create the journals and assign them to a batch as they would if workflow was not present. However, there is an additional step they will need to perform when they have finished.

Once the batch of transactions has been entered the user will need to perform the following steps to submit the batch for approval:

1. Open the **Batch Entry** window by clicking on **Batches** on the **Financials** menu under **Transactions** and then **Financial**.

2. Enter the **Batch ID** or use the lookup button to find the batch.

3. With a **General Ledger Batch Approval** workflow enabled, a new status bar is displayed below the action pane showing the current status of the batch. When a batch has been saved, but not submitted you will see the status message in the diagram above.

4. To submit the batch for approval, click the **Submit** button.

5. The **Workflow Action** window will be displayed which will allow a free form comment to be entered. Click the **Submit** button to submit the comment.

6. The batch will be submitted and the batch cleared from the window which can now be closed.

Batches can also be submitted using one of the **General Ledger Batches** navigation list. To do this, perform the following steps:

1. Click on the **Financial** series link at the bottom of the navigation pane, expand **General Ledger Batches**.

2. Click on **General Ledger Batches Not Submitted**.

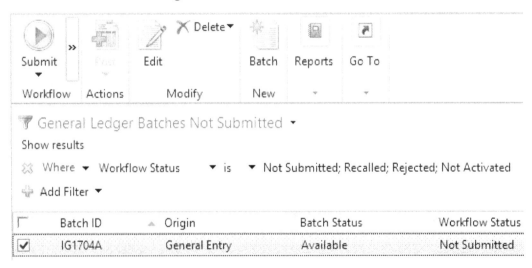

3. Mark the checkbox next to the batch to be approved.

4. Click the **Submit** button on the action pane.

5. The **Workflow Action** window will be displayed which will allow a free form comment to be entered. Click the **Submit** button to submit the comment.

Once submitted the batch will be sent to the approver(s) for review and then approval or rejection.

If you have enabled email for workflow and have marked the **Notify originator on Submit** option on the **Workflow Email Notification Maintenance** window an email will be sent to the user who submitted the batch:

Sat 21/03/2015 18:51

MDGP Workflow <mdgp-workflow@azurecurve.localdomain>

Document IG1704 has been Submitted

To   Ian Grieve

Document IG1704 has been Submitted by Ian Grieve.

User comments:
Ian Grieve, 21/03/2015 18:50:00:

Recalling a document

Once a batch has been submitted it can be recalled. Recalling a batch allows a comment to be entered against the recall and then against the next submit.

To recall a batch perform the following steps:

1. Open the **Batch Entry** window by clicking on **Batches** on the **Financials** menu under **Transactions** and then **Financial**.

2. Enter the **Batch ID** or use the lookup button to find the batch.

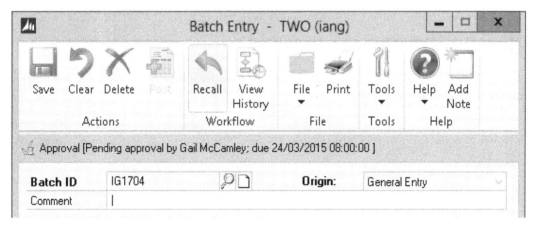

The workflow status bar will show the workflow step and who the batch has been submitted to for approval.

3. To recall the batch, click the **Recall** button.

4. The Workflow Action window will be displayed which will allow a free form comment to be entered. Click the **Recall** button to submit the message.

5. The batch will be recalled and the batch cleared from the window which can now

be closed.

Batches can also be recalled using one of the **General Ledger Batches** navigation list. To do this, perform the following steps:

1. Click on the **Financial** series link at the bottom of the navigation pane, expand **General Ledger Batches**.

2. Click on **General Ledger Batches Pending Approval**.

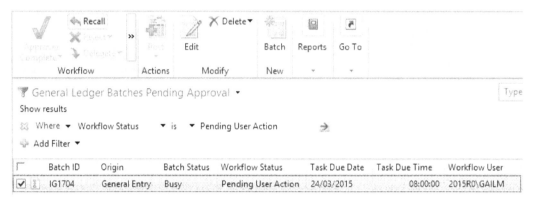

3. Mark the checkbox next to the batch to be approved.

4. Click the **Recall** button on the action pane.

5. The **Workflow Action** window will be displayed which will allow a free form comment to be entered. Click the **Submit** button to submit the comment.

Resubmitting a document

When a batch has been recalled, it will need to be resubmitted. To resubmit a batch, perform the following steps:

1. Open the **Batch Entry** window by clicking on **Batches** on the **Financials** menu under **Transactions** and then **Financial**.

2. Enter the **Batch ID** or use the lookup button to find the batch.

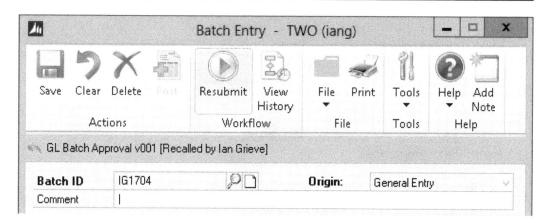

The workflow status bar will show that the batch has been recalled and who by.

3. To resubmit the batch, click the **Resubmit** button.

4. The **Workflow Action** window will be displayed which will allow a free form comment to be entered. Click the **Resubmit** button to submit the message.

5. The batch will be resubmitted and the batch cleared from the window which can now be closed.

While a recalled batch will be displayed in the **General Ledger Batches** navigation lists, they cannot be resubmitted as the button on the action pane is a **Submit** one; the **General Ledger Batches** window needs to be used to resubmit a batch..

Approving a document

Once a batch has been submitted it needs to be approved. This approval can be done through either the Microsoft Dynamics GP client (desktop or web) or through an Email Action.

Email Actions are only available if they were enabled in the Workflow Setup window (see *Chapter 2, Setting up Workflow 2.0*).

Desktop or Web Client Approval

To approve a batch through either the desktop or web client, perform the following steps:

1. Open the **Batch Entry** window by clicking on **Batches** on the **Financials** menu under **Transactions** and then **Financial**.

2. Enter the **Batch ID** or use the lookup button to find the batch.

3. Click on the Workflow button.

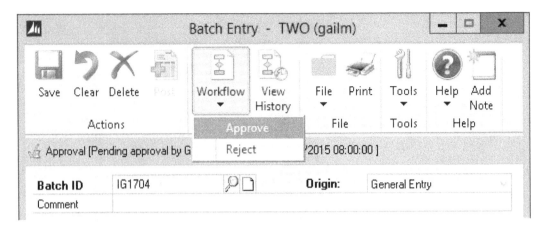

4. Click the Approve option on the drop down menu.

5. The **Workflow Action** window will be displayed which will allow a free form comment to be entered. Click the **Submit** button to submit the comment.

The General Ledger Batches Pending Approvals navigation list can be used to approve the batch. To approve the batch using the navigation list, perform the following steps:

1. Click on the **Financial** series link at the bottom of the navigation pane, expand **General Ledger Batches**.

2. Click on **General Ledger Batches Pending Approval**.

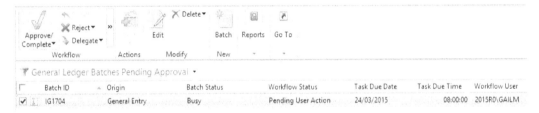

3. Mark the checkbox next to the batch to be approved.

4. Click the **Approve/Complete** button on the action pane.

5. The **Workflow Action** window will be displayed which will allow a free form comment to be entered. Click the **Submit** button to submit the comment.

If you marked the **Notify originator on Submit** in the **Workflow E-mail Notification Maintenance** window, an email will be sent confirming the approval has been performed.

Sun 22/03/2015 13:38

MDGP Workflow <mdgp-workflow@azurecurve.localdomain>

Document IG1704 has been Final Approved

To Ian Grieve

```
Document IG1704 has been Final Approved by Gail McCamley.

User comments:
Gail McCamley, 22/03/2015 13:38:00:
```

Once the batch has been approved, it can be posted as normal using one of the many options such as the Batch Entry window, the General Ledger Batches navigation list, Series or Master Posting.

Email Action Approval

If Email Actions were enabled and the Send Message checkbox marked under Assignment on the Workflow, an email will be sent to the approver which gives them options to approve, reject or delegate the document.

To approve a document using the Email Action, perform the following steps:

1. Open your email client and download emails.

2. Click the **Approve** hyperlink.

Mon 4/27/2015 5:50 AM

MDGP Workflow <mdgp-workflow@azurecurve.localdomain>

You have a task assignment for GL Batch IG1704

To Ian Grieve

```
You have been assigned a task for the Approval step in the GL Batch Approval workflow for
GL Batch IG1704.

Task Deadline: 4/27/2015 4:00:00 PM
Edit or view document: IG1704

Approve
Reject
Delegate
```

3. This will launch an Internet Explorer window using the **Web Services for Microsoft Dynamics GP**. Enter an optional **Comment**.

4. Click the **Approve** button.

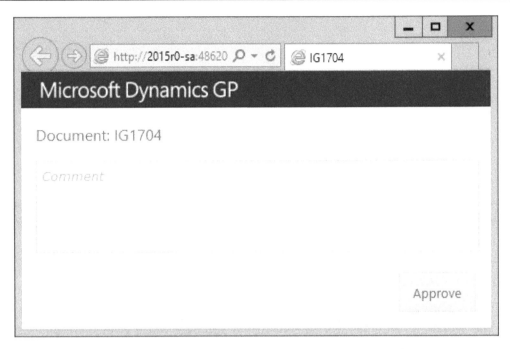

5. After the approval confirmation is displayed, close the IE window.

Rejecting a document

An alternative to approving the batch, is to reject it. As with approvals, rejections can also be done two ways; through either the client (desktop or web) or by an Email Action.

Desktop or Web Client Rejection

Rejecting a batch in the desktop or web client can be done by performing the following steps:

1. Open the **Batch Entry** window by clicking on **Batches** on the **Financials** menu under **Transactions** and then **Financial**.

2. Enter the **Batch ID** or use the lookup button to find the batch.

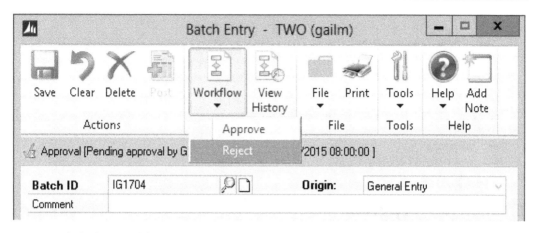

3. Click the Workflow button.

4. Click the Reject option on the dropdown list.

5. The **Workflow Action** window will be displayed which will allow a free form comment to be entered. Click the **Submit** button to submit the comment.

As with the approval, the General Ledger Batches Pending Approvals navigation list can be used to reject the batch. To reject the batch using the navigation list, perform the following steps:

1. Click on the **Financial** series link at the bottom of the navigation pane and expand **General Ledger Batches.**

2. Click on **General Ledger Batches Pending Approval**.

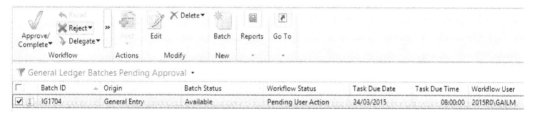

3. Mark the checkbox next to the batch to be rejected.

4. Click the **Reject** button on the action pane.

5. The **Workflow Action** window will be displayed which will allow a free form comment to be entered. Click the **Reject** button to submit the comment.

If you marked the **Notify originator on Reject** in the **Workflow E-mail Notification Maintenance** window, an email will be sent confirming the submit has been performed.

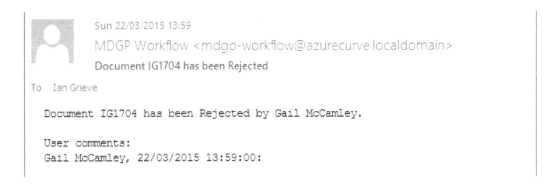

Sun 22/03/2015 13:59

MDGP Workflow <mdgp-workflow@azurecurve.localdomain>
Document IG1704 has been Rejected

To   Ian Grieve

Document IG1704 has been Rejected by Gail McCamley.

User comments:
Gail McCamley, 22/03/2015 13:59:00:

Email Action Rejection

When Email Actions are being used the rejection can also be done from email. To reject using the Email Action, perform the following steps:

1. Open your email client and download emails.

2. Click the **Reject** hyperlink.

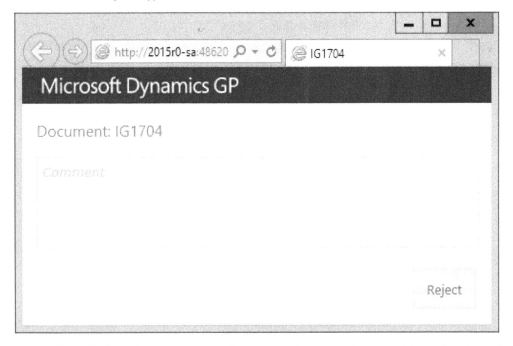

3. This will launch an Internet Explorer window using the **Web Services for Microsoft Dynamics GP**. Enter an optional **Comment**.

4. Click the **Reject** button.

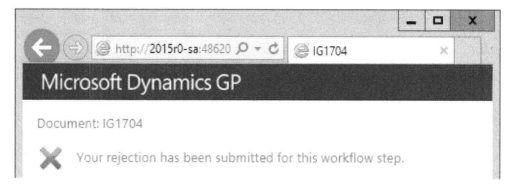

5. After the approval confirmation is displayed, close the IE window.

The selected action is not available

If a user clicks an approval hyperlink for a document which has already been Final Approved, or Rejected, they will receive a warning message.

Email Action Failure

Experience has shown that it is common for the E-Mail Actions to result in a Request Error.

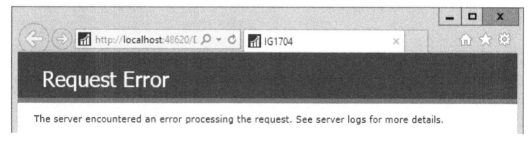

This error can be avoided by adding English (United States) as a language within the Internet Options (it does not need to be the default, only added as a language). Unfortunately this needs to be done on every client.

1. Launch an Internet Explorer window and click on **Internet Options** under the **Settings** icon.

2. Under **Accessibility** click the **Languages** button to open the Language Preference window.

3. Click the **Set Language Preferences** button to open the **Language** window.

4. Click the **Add a language** button on the toolbar.

5. In the **Add Languages** window, scroll down to the **E**'s and select **English** and then click the **Open** button.

6. Select **English (United States)** and click **Add**.

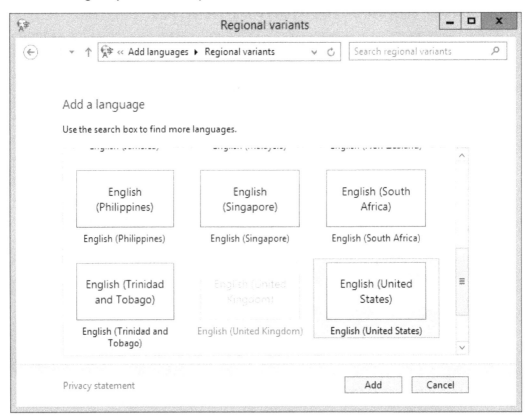

7. Close the **Language** window using the cross in the top right corner.

8. Click **OK** to close the **Language Preference**.

9. Click **OK** to close the **Internet Options**.

Delegating a task

When a batch has been submitted for approval, there are three actions which can be taken against it. The first two, approval and rejection, have been covered already; the third action is delegation.

This is where the approval user can delegate the approval/rejection to another user. This is useful if the batch being approved is for a particular reason which the main approver has no responsibility for and wants to pass the batch to another user who does work in this area.

Delegation can also be performed in the desktop, or web, client or via an Email Action.

Desktop or Web Client Delegation

To delegate a batch in the desktop or web client, perform the following steps:

1. Open the **Batch Entry** window by clicking on **Batches** on the **Financials** menu under **Transactions** and then **Financial**.

2. Enter the **Batch ID** or use the lookup button to find the batch

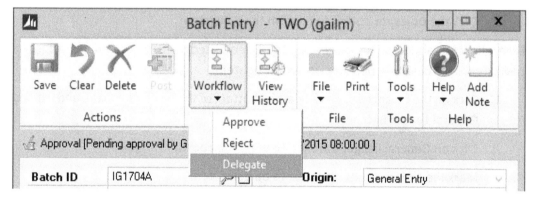

3. Click the **Workflow** button.

4. A dropdown menu will appear below the **Workflow** button, click on **Delegate**.

5. The **Workflow Action** window which is displayed, contains a **Delegate to** lookup field at the top. Enter the name of the user and click the binoculars button to perform a lookup on Active Directory.

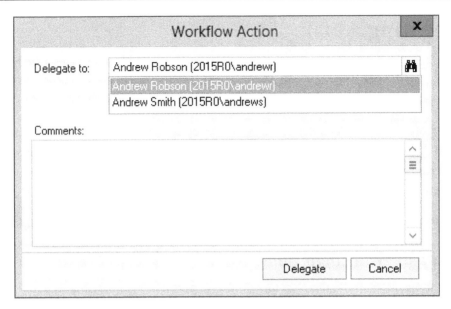

6. Select the user you want to delegate the approval from the list of users; the first user returned is selected by default.

7. Enter a comment in the **Comment** field as to why the approval is being delegated.

8. Click the **Delegate** button to confirm the delegation.

Delegation can also be performed from the General Ledger Batches Pending Approval navigation list. To do this, perform the following steps:

1. Click on the **Financial** series link at the bottom of the navigation pane and expand **General Ledger Batches.**

2. Click on **General Ledger Batches Pending Approval**.

3. Mark the checkbox next to batch to be delegated.

4. Click the **Delegate** button on the action pane.

5. A window will popup below the **Delegate** button; in the **Delegate to** field enter the name of the user and click the binoculars button.

6. A list of users matching the entered name will be displayed for you to select the required user; by default the first returned user name is selected.

7. Enter a reason for the delegation in the **Comment** field.

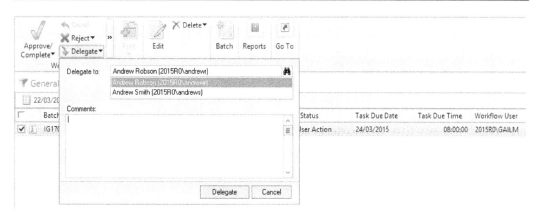

8. Click **Delegate** to confirm the delegation.

Email Action Delegation

When Email Actions are being used the rejection can also be done from email. To reject using the Email Action, perform the following steps:

1. Open your email client and download emails.

2. Click the **Delegate** hyperlink.

3. This will launch an Internet Explorer window using the **Web Services for Microsoft Dynamics GP**.

4. In the Delegate field enter the name of the user to whom the task should be delegated. A lookup will be performed on active directory; select the user you want from the list.

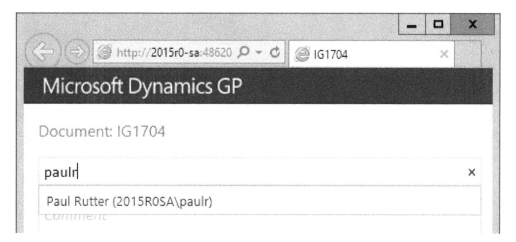

5. Enter an optional **Comment;** I typically recommend entering a comment for delegation where for approval and rejection it isn't as necessary. Entering a comment for the delegation, allows the recipient to know why the task was delegated.

6. Click the **Delegate** button.

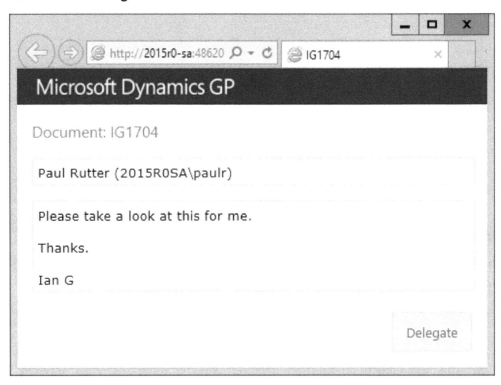

7. After the delegation confirmation is displayed, close the IE window.

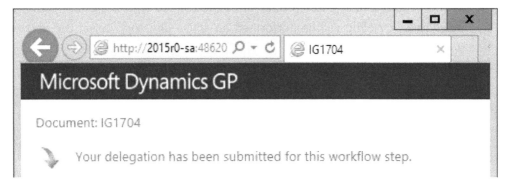

8. An email will be sent to the user receiving the delegation which allows them to approve, reject or even delegate the approval again should there be a need.

Mon 4/27/2015 5:58 AM

MDGP Workflow <mdgp-workflow@azurecurve.localdomain>

You have a task assignment for GL Batch IG1704

To   Paul Rutter

You have been assigned a task for the Approval step in the GL Batch Approval workflow for
GL Batch IG1704.

Task Deadline: 4/27/2015 4:00:00 PM
Edit or view document: IG1704

Approve
Reject
Delegate

Batch ID: IG1704
Comment:
Origin: GL_Normal
Journal Entries: 1
Batch Total: 200.00000

Comments:
Ian Grieve, 4/27/2015 5:50:00 AM:

Ian Grieve, 4/27/2015 5:55:00 AM: Delegated to: Paul Rutter. Please take a look at this for
me.

Thanks.

Ian G

Automatically delegating a task

As well as manually delegating a task, automatic delegation can also be configured. This
is useful for times when you will be unavailable. For example, when off on holiday or out
on site for a few days.

This is done in the Workflow User Delegation window accessible via the User Preferences
window. Workflow Delegation can be configured for all workflow types or individual ones;
if delegation for individual workflows is configured a different user can be selected for
each one.

To configure automatic delegation, perform the following steps:

1. Click the **Microsoft Dynamics GP menu** and then on **User Preferences**.

2. Click on the **Workflow Delegation** button to open the **Workflow User Delegation**
    window.

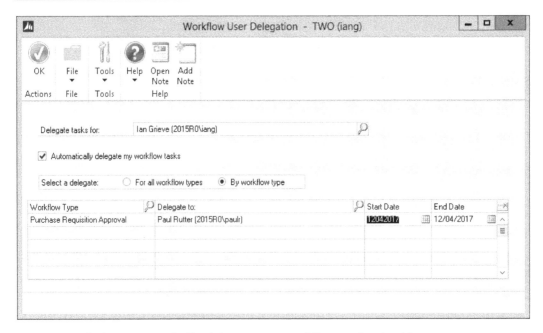

3. Mark the **Automatically delegate my workflow tasks** checkbox.

4. In **Select a delegate**, mark the **By workflow type** radio button.

5. Click the lookup button next to the **Workflow Type** header in the scrolling window to open the **Workflow Types** window.

6. In the list of **Workflow Types**, select the desired **Workflow Type**.

7. Click **Select** to select the workflow and close the **Workflow Types** window.

8. Either enter the user name of the user to delegate to or use the lookup button and do a search.

9. Enter a date in the **Start Date** field for the date from which to start delegating.

10. Enter a date in the **End Date** field for the date on which delegation should be ended.

11. Repeat steps 5 through 10 for additional **Workflow Types**.

12. Click **OK** to save the changes and close the **Workflow User Delegation** window.

13. Click **OK** to close the **User Preferences** window.

Viewing the Workflow History

After being submitted for the first time, workflow processes can pass through various different steps.

For example, some might be submitted and then immediately approved; alternatively, they might be submitted, recalled, resubmitted, rejected, resubmitted, delegated and approved.

One of the useful pieces of functionality that Workflow 2.0 has, is that you can view the workflow history of a batch. The history can be viewed at any stage of the process. For example, there is a View History button on the General Ledger Batch Entry window and also, as shown below, on the Journal Entry Inquiry window:

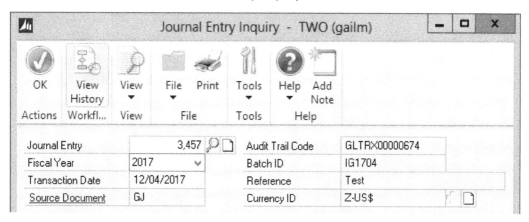

Clicking this button will launch the Workflow History window which shows the detailed history of the batch as it interacts with workflow.

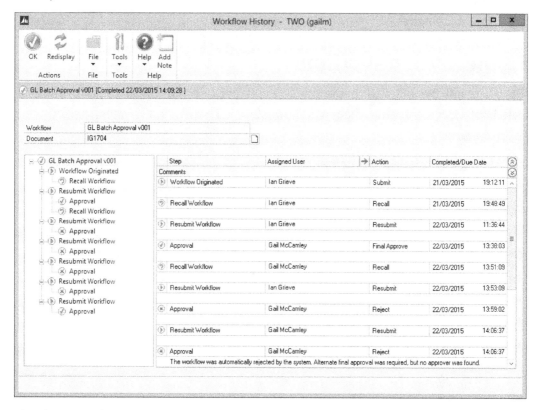

The diagram above shows the history of batch IG1704 which I have been using as the example in this chapter. The navigation pane on the left of the window shows the different interactions; the detail pane on the right shows the detail of these interactions including the Step, Assigned User, Action and the Completion/Due Date.

You'll see that each of the workflow action types are accompanied by an icon which are described below:

- **Submitted**

- **Recalled**

- **Resubmitted**

- **Pending Approval**

- **Approved**

- **Rejected**

- **Delegated**

Escalated – this is an automatic action which workflow performs when the assigned user has failed to action the approval or task step by the deadline.

Task Complete – this icon is displayed for **Task** steps and not the **Approval** type step created in this chapter.

Home screen sections

The Microsoft Dynamics GP home screen has several sections available, which display details of documents and their workflow status. To enable a section, perform the following steps:

1. Log into **Microsoft Dynamics** GP.

2. In the top right corner of the home screen, click on **Customize** this screen.

3. Mark the following sections as appropriate:

    a. **Time Management**;

    b. **Procurement**;

    c. **Project Time & Expense**.

A panel will be displayed for each section which allows for interaction with items of the relevant type.

A section will include the standard Microsoft Design Language tile (formerly known as Metro) as well as text links and a list of transactions.

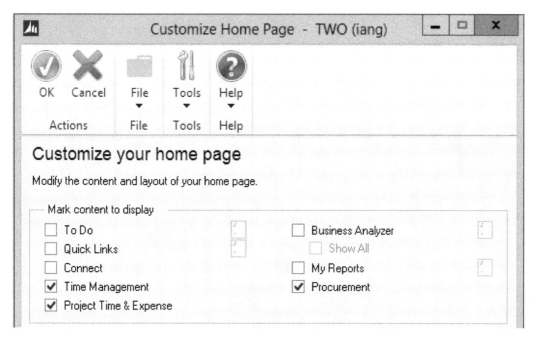

Each transaction type will include a section and links appropriate to the type. The below example is for Procurement.

Summary

In this chapter we have taken a look at how users will interact with the batch as it moves through the process defined in the workflow. In the next chapter, we'll take a look at creating a more complex workflow process.

6

Creating a Complex Purchase Requisition Approval Workflow

In this chapter we're going to take a look at creating a more complex workflow process than we looked at in Chapter 4. In this chapter, we'll be creating a Purchase Requisition Approval workflow covering several directorates, each with different rules surrounding the approval.

The workflow process we created in *Chapter 4, Creating a Simple Batch Approval Workflow*, was a very simple one with only a single step. However, workflow processes can be far more complex. For the complex workflows, I would strongly recommend planning your workflow process before starting to create it.

Tools such as Microsoft Visio are good for creating this type of diagram; I used the Basic Flowchart type which is good for designing process flows.

Designing the Workflow

When working with clients to implement Workflow 2.0, there are two documents we typically create to assist the creation and also to satisfy the auditor requirements.

The first document is the Design Document which contains the business requirements and is written in language non-technical people will understand. The key element of the design document is the design diagram which is a visual representation of the proposed workflow.

This diagram gives users the ability to understand how the workflow will function. For complex workflows, this is typically not a single diagram, but a series of diagrams with each representing the first decision point which, based on experience so far, is usually a department, directorate or cost center.

Gathering Requirements

The first step in designing a workflow process, is to gather the business requirements. The purchase requisition approval workflow example I am going to cover in this chapter is for Perfect Image.

The requirements from the business is that each department has its own approvers and, depending on value, there may be two levels of approval required.

Design Diagram

Rather than designing a single design diagram for all departments, I would recommend multiple design diagrams with one for each department, but with the diagram containing the department decision step. The design diagram below, is the one for the ERP Practice.

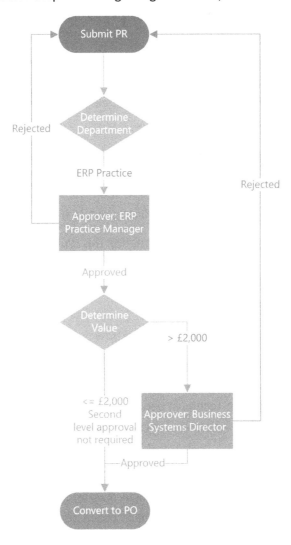

The workflow process starts with a purchase requisition being entered into the system and submitted for approval. All purchase requisitions for the ERP Practice go to the ERP Practice Manager for approval.

Perfect Image doesn't have a high turnover of staff, so the department will be determined by the user who placed the requisition. This is determined by the Requested By field which is automatically set to the User Id of the user who entered the requisition. If using the Requested By was not suitable, we could have used User-Defined 1 and had the user enter the department; to enforce this, Modifier could have been used to make the field mandatory.

After this first level of approval, there is a decision step to determine the value; if the value is less than or equal to £2,000 then second level approval is required. If the value is greater than £2,000, approval from the Business Systems Director is also required.

Similar design diagrams would be produced for the other departments, such as the CRM Practice, Development, Infrastructure, Service Desk and so on.

These design diagrams would form part of the larger design document which is distributed to the business decision makers for approval. Each department could have a slightly different processes; for example, the CRM Practice may have different approval levels or the Service Desk three levels of approval required for certain values.

Build Diagram

The design diagram I covered in the previous section, is effective as part of the design document in being understandable by non-technical users and allowing them to review and approve the design for implementation.

This document, however, is not suitable for using when building the workflow process in the Microsoft Dynamics GP Workflow Maintenance window.

The design diagram has to be interpreted and understood for the build to be completed and this is not always straightforward to accomplish. Instead I would recommend the creation of a build document, the main part of which is the build diagram.

The build document would detail how transactions are to be entered, if any customizations are required (such as making a field, such as User-Defined 1, mandatory).

The build diagram is created in such a way that it can be handed to someone with no knowledge of the project to complete the build. It is structured and written so that the person doing the build merely needs to transpose from the build diagram into Workflow Maintenance.

In the design diagram there is a **Determine Department** decision, but with how Workflow

2.0 works, you cannot actually create a decision step of this type.

A workflow step has a parent and can use **Conditions** to determine who should be assigned the approval; but, this in effect only allows one leg. So the **Condition** to determine the team is actually part of the step itself.

The design diagram is drawn this way as people understand this type of flow chart so they can understand it for approving the design.

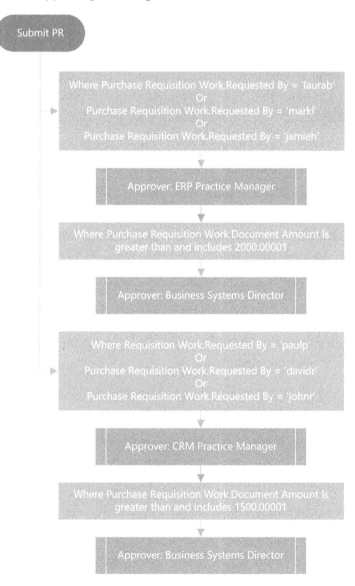

Assign the managers

As mentioned in the last chapter, all Workflow Types need to have at least one manager assigned. To assign managers, perform the following steps:

1. Open the **Workflow Maintenance** window by clicking **Workflow Maintenance** from the **Administration menu** under **Setup** and **Company**.

2. **Purchasing** is the default Workflow Type when the window opens; there are four types of workflow available under **Purchasing**, so you will need to select **Purchase Requisition Approval** from the list to populate the detail pane.

3. Click the lookup button next to the multiline **Managers** field to open the **Workflow User Selection** window.

4. Type the name of the first manager and click the lookup button; this will perform a lookup on Active Directory and pull back the details of the related username.

   If there was more than one username returned, click on the user you want.

5. Click the **Add** button to add the user to the **Selected Users list**.

6. Repeat steps 2 through 4 to add any additional managers.

7. Click the **OK** button to save the changes and close the **Workflow User Selection** window.

8. Click the **Save Type** button on the action pane to save the changes to the managers.

Create the workflow process

The workflow process we're going to create in this chapter is a more complex one than the GL approval one we created earlier, but, as mentioned, the process for creating the workflow is the same.

To create a workflow process, perform the following steps:

1. Open the Workflow Maintenance window by clicking Workflow Maintenance from the **Administration menu** under **Setup** and **Company**.

2. **Purchasing** is the Workflow Type displayed by default; click on **Purchase Requisition Approval** will be automatically selected and displayed in the detail pane.

3. Click the **New Workflow** button on the action pane; this will change the content of the detail pane to show the Workflow layout.

4. Enter the name of the workflow in the **Workflow Name** field. I have entered `Purchase Requisition v001`.

Workflow Name	Purchase Requisition v001	☐	☐ Active
Description	Purchase Requisition v001		
Workflow Type	Purchase Requisition Approval		

5. The **Description** field can contain a longer description of the intent of the workflow process, but I have opted to set it the same as the **Workflow Name** field.

6. Mark the **Send notifications for completed actions** checkbox.

7. Click the blue expansion arrow button to open the **Workflow Email Notification Maintenance** window.

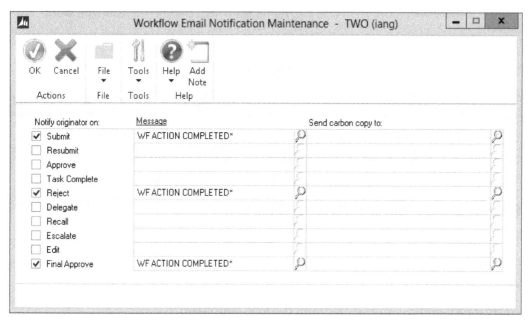

8. Mark the **Submit**, **Reject** and **Final Approve** checkboxes; if only one **Message ID** for each type of action exists, this will be defaulted into the **Message** field, otherwise you will need to click the lookup button and select the required Message ID.

9. Click **OK** to close the **Workflow Email Notification Maintenance** window.

10. Mark the **Allow approver to delegate tasks** checkbox to allow the approver to send tasks to other people to complete.

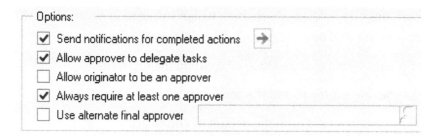

11. Mark the **Always require at least one approver**.

12. Click the **Save Workflow** button on the action pane to save the newly created workflow process.

Create the workflow steps

The Purchase Approval Requisition workflow we are creating in this chapter will consist of more steps than the single-step General Ledger Batch Approval workflow we created in the previous chapter.

ERP Practice Approval Step

To create the **ERP Practice Approval** step, perform the following actions:

1. Click the **New Step** button on the action pane.

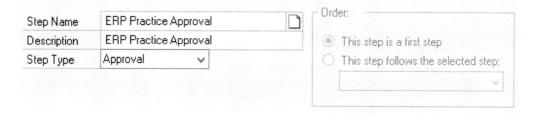

2. Enter ERP Practice Approval in the **Step Name** and **Description** fields.

3. Under the **Condition** header, mark the Acti**on is required only when the following condition is met**.

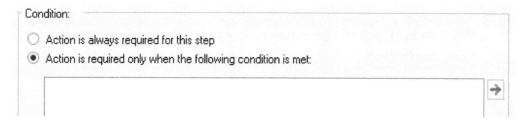

4. Click the blue expansion arrow button to the right of the frame to open the **Workflow Condition Editor** window.

5. Leave the first field at where and change the second to **Purchase Requisition Work.Requested By**.

6. Set the third field to **is** and type `laurab` in the fourth field.

7. Click the **Add** button to add the condition.

8. Change the first field from the default of **and** to **or**.

9. If you are using Microsoft Dynamics GP 2013 R2 be aware that the **or** operator did not work correctly; this bug was fixed in Microsoft Dynamics GP 2015.

10. Set the second field to **Purchase Requisition Work.Requested By**.

11. Leave the third field set to **is** and enter the user id of the next user.

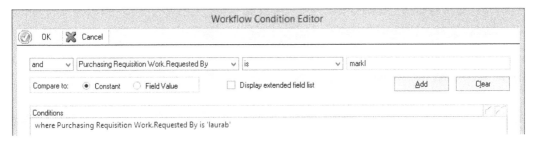

12. Click **Add** to add the condition.

13. Repeat steps 9 to 12 for each additional user.

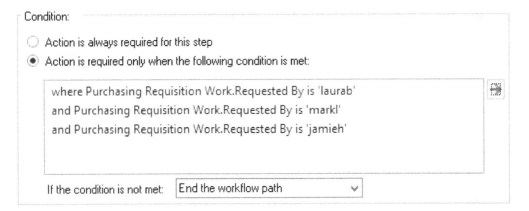

14. When finished, click the **OK** button to save the changes and close the **Workflow Condition Editor**.

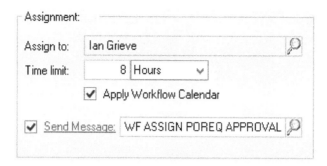

15. Under **Assignment**, select the user(s) who need to approve this step; in this case, I have selected myself.

16. Set the **Time limit** to the required time; I wanted to set the length as one working day, but the length can only be round units of time so I have selected 8 **Hours**.

17. Click the **Save Step** button on the action pane.

ERP Practice > £2,000

As with the **Determine Team** decision step, the **ERP Price > £2,000** step is not one that you create within Workflow 2.0, but instead the value check is the condition in the **ERP Practice Director Approval** step itself; if a purchase requisition line's extended cost is less than £2,00 then the workflow approval process is complete and the purchase requisition can be converted to a purchase order.

ERP Practice Director Approval Step

To create the **ERP Practice Director Approval** step, perform the following steps:

1. Click the **New Step** button on the action pane.

2. In the **Step Name** field enter ERP Practice Director Approval.

3. In the **Description** enter ERP Practice Approval where Price > £2,000.

4. If the **ERP Practice Approval** step was the selected step when you clicked the **New Step** button it will be set as the step the **ERP Practice Director Approval** step follows; if it wasn't then mark the This step follows the selected step and select **ERP Practice Approval** in the dropdown list.

5. Mark the **Action is required only when the following condition is met** checkbox and click the expansion arrow to open the **Workflow Condition Editor** window.

6. Leave the first field set to **where**.

7. Select **Purchasing Requisition Line.Extended Cost** from the list of available fields.

8. Change the third field to is **greater than and includes**.

9. Click the **Add** button to add the condition.

10. Click **OK** to save the change and close the **Workflow Condition Editor**.

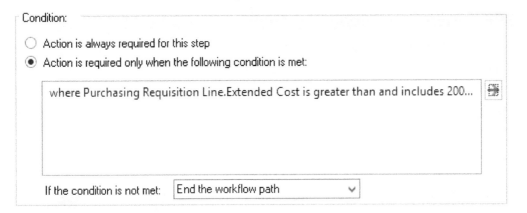

11. The final part of the configuration of this step is to configure the **Assignment**. Select the user(s) who will approve this step.

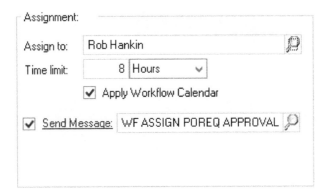

12. Set the **Time limit** to the required time.

13. Click the **Save Step** button on the action pane

CRM Practice Approval

The **CRM Practice** leg of this example workflow process is created in exactly the same way as the **ERP Practice** leg. The only difference is in the names, selected users, approvers and the price at which director approval is required.

Review the workflow process steps

As you create the workflow steps you can use the navigation pane on the Workflow Maintenance window to make sure that steps are created in the correct order. If you have followed the build diagram then the steps you see in the list should match the diagram; clicking on one of the steps will allow you to review the conditions which have been created. Again, if you created the build diagram using the same, or similar, format as the one I use, you should be able to match the steps in workflow against the build diagram.

Activate the workflow process

Now that the workflow process has been configured for both the ERP and CRM Practices, the workflow process needs to be activated. To do this, perform the following steps:

1. Open the Workflow Maintenance window by clicking Workflow Maintenance from the **Administration menu** under **Setup** and **Company**.

2. Expand **Purchase Requisition Approval** in the navigation tree.

3. Load the workflow process by clicking on **Purchase Requisition v001**.

4. Mark the **Active** checkbox in the top right of the window next to the **Workflow Name** field.

5. Click the **Save Workflow** button on the action pane.

6. Close the **Workflow Maintenance** window.

Summary

In this chapter we have taken a look at creating a more complex workflow process than we did in Chapter 4. Being a complex workflow process does not equate to being complicated; the steps needed for creating a complex workflow are just the same as creating a simple one.

There are two key points to remember when designing a workflow process. Firstly, there are no decision steps which allow a branching down different legs. Secondly, a step can have only one parent so you cannot have branches coming together.

The reason I mention this is that both might be included in a design diagram, such as the one I showed at the start of this chapter, but cannot be created in Workflow 2.0.

In the next chapter, we'll cover the creation of a non-transactional workflow process; a Vendor Approval workflow.

7

Creating a Vendor Approval Workflow

The two workflows I have covered so far, General Ledger Batch Approval and Purchase Requisition Approval are both document based ones, so, in this chapter, I am going to create a non-document related workflow.

There are several non-document workflows of which I am going to cover the Vendor Approval one. This workflow requires any newly created vendor or amended vendor to be approved before transactions can be posted; they can be entered and saved.

The approval process for a non-document based workflow process is exactly the same as a document based one. The approval/rejection can be done via either the Vendor Maintenance window or via a navigation list in Purchasing.

Before you begin

As discussed in the last chapter, before starting to create a Vendor Approval workflow, it is best to draw a workflow diagram to ensure the workflow is built to meet the requirements. If we assume that the company we are working with, in this example Fabrikam, Inc., is a multinational then we may want to assign different approvers for the different regions.

We could also make the workflow more complex by adding additional checks which then requires either additional approval levels or different approvers. One such example, might be to include a check on the Credit Limit so vendors with a higher credit limit need to be approved by someone more senior.

The flowchart, below, shows the fairly simple workflow we will build in this chapter, where approval has been broken down into two geographic regions (Americas and Australia) using the Vendor Class IDs to differentiate vendors by region.

Because this is a small, simple, workflow process, I have included both results of the Determine Region decision step in the one diagram, rather than breaking it down as I did in the Purchase Requisition Approval workflow created in an earlier chapter.

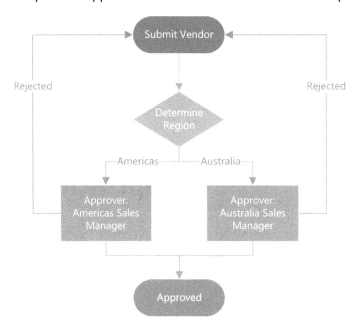

As the design diagram is a simple one, the build diagram for the above design diagram is also a simple one.

Assign the managers

As we have done with the other workflow types, at least one manager must be assigned to the Vendor Approval workflow type. To assign managers, perform the following steps:

1. Open the **Workflow Maintenance** window by clicking **Workflow Maintenance** from the **Administration menu** under **Setup** and **Company**.

2. **Purchasing** is the default Workflow Type when the window opens; there are four types of workflow available under **Purchasing**, so you will need to select **Vendor Approval** from the list to populate the detail pane.

3. Click the lookup button next to the multiline **Managers** field to open the **Workflow User Selection** window.

4. Type the name of the first manager and click the lookup button; this will perform a lookup on Active Directory and pull back the details of the related username.

   If there was more than one username returned, click on the user you want.

5. Click the **Add** button to add the user to the **Selected Users list**.

6. Repeat steps 2 through 4 to add any additional managers.

7. Click the **OK** button to save the changes and close the **Workflow User Selection** window.

8. Click the **Save Type** button on the action pane to save the changes to the managers.

Create the workflow process

Now we have designed the workflow process and assigned managers, we can create the workflow by performing the following steps:

1. Open the Workflow Maintenance window by clicking Workflow Maintenance from the **Administration menu** under **Setup** and **Company**.

2. **Purchasing** is the **Workflow Type** displayed by default; click on **Vendor Approval** to load it into the detail pane.

3. Click the **New Workflow** button on the action pane; this will change the content of the detail pane to show the Workflow layout.

4. Enter the name of the workflow, `Vendor Approval v001`, in the **Workflow Name** field.

Workflow Name	Vendor Approval v001	🗋	☐ Active
Description	Vendor Approval by Region		
Workflow Type	Vendor Approval	⌄	

5. Enter `Vendor Approval by Region`, in the **Description** field.

6. Mark the **Send notifications for completed actions** and click the expansion button to open the **Workflow Email Notification Maintenance** window.

7. Mark the checkboxes next to **Reject** and **Final Approve**.

8. Click **OK** to save the changes and close the **Workflow Email Notification Maintenance** window.

9. Mark the **Allow approver to delegate tasks** and **Always require at least one approver** checkboxes.

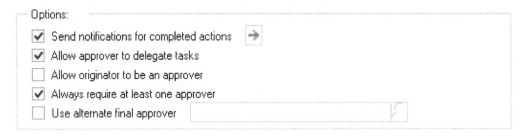

10. Click the **Save Workflow** button to save the workflow and enable the **New Workflow** button.

Create the workflow steps

This Vendor Approval workflow is a simple one which does not have many steps.

Determine Region

Although the workflow diagram shows a determine region decision step, Workflow 2.0 does not support the creation of this type of step. Instead the Conditions are used to configure this within each step.

Americas Approval

The first step we will create is the Americas Approval step. To create this step, perform the following actions:

1. Click the **New Step** button.

2. Enter Americas Approval in the **Step Name** field.

3. Enter Approval of Americas Based Vendors in the **Description** field.

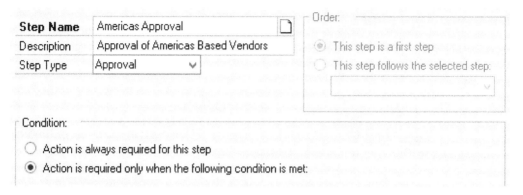

4. Mark the **Action is required only when the following condition is met** radio button.

5. Click the expansion button to open the **Workflow Condition Editor** window.

6. Set the second field to **Vendor Master.Vendor Class ID**.

7. Change the third field to **begins with**.

8. Enter USA in the fourth field.

9. Click **Add** to add the selection to the **Conditions** list.

10. Repeat steps 6 through 9 to add **Vendor Class IDs** beginning with CAN.

11. Click **OK** to save the changes and close the **Workflow Condition Editor** window.

12. Select a user to **Assign to** for the approver.

13. Set a **Time limit** and mark the **Apply Workflow Calendar** checkbox.

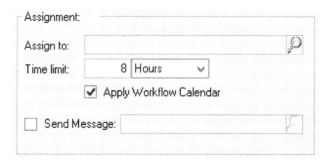

14. Click the **Save Step** button on the action pane.

Australia Approval

The second step is the Australia Approval step which can be created following these steps:

1. Click the **New Step** button.

2. Enter `Australia Approval` in the **Step Name** field.

3. Enter `Approval of Australia Based Vendors` in the **Description** field. Mark the This step is a first step radio button.

4. Mark the **Action is required only when the following condition is met** radio button.

5. Click the expansion button to open the **Workflow Condition Editor** window.

6. Set the second field to **Vendor Master.Vendor Class ID**.

7. Change the third field to **begins with**.

8. Enter `AUS` in the fourth field.

9. Click **Add** to add the selection to the **Conditions** list.

10. Repeat steps 6 through 9 to add **Vendor Class IDs** beginning with `NEW`.

11. Click **OK** to save the changes and close the **Workflow Condition Editor** window.

12. Select a user to **Assign to** for the approver.

13. Set a **Time limit** and mark the **Apply Workflow Calendar** checkbox.

14. Click the **Save Step** button on the action pane.

Activate the workflow process

Now that the workflow process has been configured for both regions, the workflow process needs to be activated. To do this, perform the following steps:

1. Open the Workflow Maintenance window by clicking Workflow Maintenance from the **Administration menu** under **Setup** and **Company**.

2. Expand **Vendor Approval** in the navigation tree.

3. Load the workflow process by clicking on Vendor Approval v001.

4. Mark the **Active** checkbox in the top right of the window next to the **Workflow Name** field.

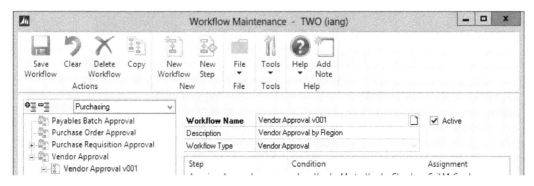

5. Click the **Save Workflow** button on the action pane.

6. Close the **Workflow Maintenance** window.

Testing the Vendor Approval workflow

The approval of a Vendor Change workflow is done in the same way as a document based one; it can be done via the buttons on the Vendor Maintenance window or one of the supplied navigation lists.

To test the **Vendor Approval** workflow process, either create a new vendor or change an existing one and save the record without submitting the change.

When you try to post an invoice for this creditor the following message will be confirmed:

Now submit the change for approval via the **Vendor Maintenance** card or the **Vendors Not Submitted** workflow.

If you try to post the invoice, before the change is approved the following message will be displayed:

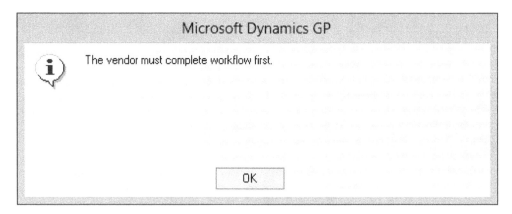

If you now approve the submitted vendor you will be able to successfully post the invoice.

Summary

In this chapter we have taken a look at creating a Vendor Approval workflow based on the Vendor Class ID assigned to the vendors. We also took a look at how users interact with this type of workflow process. In the next chapter, we'll be taking a look at adding additional tables for workflow conditions.

8

Adding Additional Tables for Workflow Conditions

Workflow 2.0 allows conditions to be set for workflow steps using any field which is on the document type. However, when developing workflows, the available fields for setting conditions are not always sufficient to meet the requirements. Only fields which are directly on the document can be used for setting a condition. For example, a workflow for Receivables Transaction Approval cannot be based on debtor class because the class is not stored on the transaction, but on the debtor itself and so is not listed as an available field for setting conditions.

In addition, in many transaction based workflows, such as ones for purchase requisitions or purchase orders, the requirement may be to create a condition based on a segment of the account.

Unfortunately, the condition will not work as expected because the condition is actually being compared against the account index, instead of against the account; in the case of a purchase requisition or purchase order, the Inventory Index.

Both of the above issues are solvable. This is possible because Workflow 2.0 does support the ability to make additional fields available for setting conditions, by adding additional tables into the condition editor for the workflow type.

The tool used for this was originally created to facilitate the creation of new workflow types, but can also be used to modify existing workflow types. If you look for this functionality in a standard deploy of Microsoft Dynamics GP, you will not find it, as it is hidden from view.

Making the enhanced Workflow Condition Editor Visible

The enhanced Workflow Condition Editor is hidden by default, as it is a tool which needs to be handled with care, as incautious use can break workflow. As such, it should only be enabled while performing the work of adding additional tables to the workflow type, and then switched off afterwards.

The relationships for the tables and fields used for setting workflow conditions are stored within the company database. One important point to note, is that there is no undo function available. If a relationship is corrupted or invalid, the workflow type will cease to work and a manual correction will be required.

There are two recommendations which should be followed before updating the workflow table relationships on a production system:

1. Update and test the new or updated relationships on a test company before making the change in a production one.

2. Ensure a good backup has been taken of the production company before making any changes and test the changes before allowing users to log back in.

To enable the enhanced Workflow Condition Editor, perform the following steps:

1. Exit Dynamics GP if you are logged in (and if using a terminal or XenApp server get all other users out).

2. Edit the **Dex.ini** file, located in **%ProgramFiles(x86)%\Microsoft Dynamics\GP 2016\Data** by default, and add the following line under the **[General]** heading:

QueryDesignerAllFunctionality=TRUE

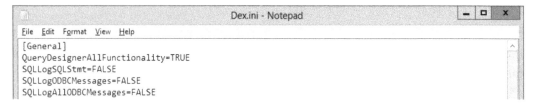

3. Launch **Microsoft Dynamics GP** and log into a test company.

4. In the **Navigation** pane click on **Administration** and then under **Setup** and **Company**, click on **Workflow**.

5. Select a **Workflow Type** and workflow process.

6. Select a step and click the expansion arrow next to the **Condition** list to open the **Workflow Condition Editor**.

7. If the enhanced **Workflow Condition Editor** has been correctly enabled you should see a window like the one below:

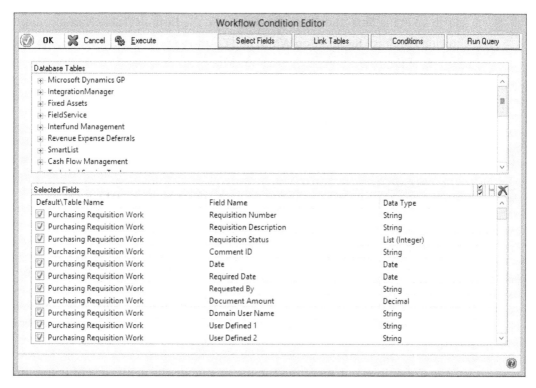

With the enhanced Workflow Condition Editor enabled, the table relationships and available fields can be added or updated.

Updating tables on the Purchase Requisition Approval Workflow Type

Before we look at adding new table relationships into a workflow type, we will first take a look at updating existing tables. This is sometimes necessary as not all of the fields from a table contained within a workflow type were exposed by Microsoft.

To make these fields available, the enhanced Workflow Condition Editor can be used. To make the Country Code from the purchase requisition and the Currency ID from the purchase requisition lines available as conditions, follow these steps:

1. Open **Workflow Maintenance** from the **Administration** area page under **Setup** and **Company** by clicking on **Workflow**.

2. Expand the **Purchase Requisition Approval** node in the workflow type list.

3. Create a new workflow, as described in *Chapter 6, Creating a Complex Purchase Requisition Workflow*.

4. When creating the first step, open the **Workflow Condition Editor**, which will open with the **Select Fields** tab visible.

5. Scroll down in the **Selected Fields** list and, while the **Default\Table Name** column is showing **Purchase Requisition Work**, find **Country Code** and mark the checkbox to the left of the row.

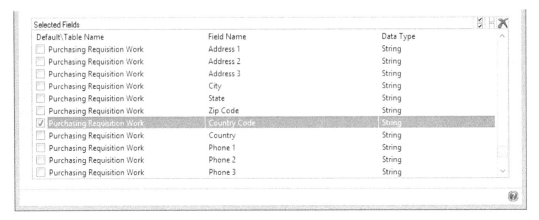

6. Scroll down further and, while the **Default\Table Name** column is showing **Purchase Requisition Line**, find **Currency ID** and mark the checkbox to the left of the row.

7. Click the **Conditions** button of the toolbar to change the view and configure the required conditions; the newly selected fields will display in the field list for selection:

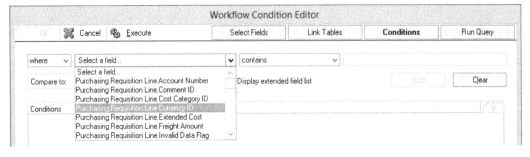

Once additional fields have been selected, they are available for all workflow steps and also for all workflows of the type to which they were added.

Adding table relationships on the Purchase Requisition Approval Workflow Type

In addition to adding extra fields from existing tables, it is also possible to use the enhanced Workflow Condition Editor window to add new table relationships. Possibly the most common reason for doing this is to allow the account to be used in a purchase requisition workflow.

To add a new relationship to the Account Master table, perform the following steps:

8. Open **Workflow Maintenance** from the **Administration** area page under **Setup** and **Company** by clicking on **Workflow**.

1. Expand the **Purchase Requisition Approval** node in the workflow type list.

2. Create a new workflow, as described in *Chapter 6, Creating a Complex Purchase Requisition Workflow*, or open an existing one.

3. When creating, or editing, the first step, open the **Workflow Condition Editor**, which will open with the **Select Fields** tab visible.

4. In the **Database Tables** list, expand the **Microsoft Dynamics GP** node.

9. Expand the **Financial** and **Account Master** nodes.

5. Mark the checkbox next to the **Account Number** field; this will automatically add a mark in the **Account Master** table node.

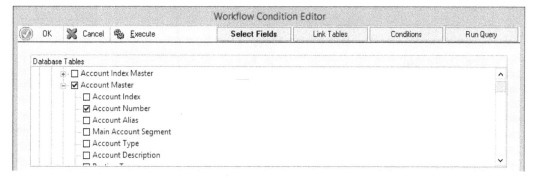

6. Mark the checkbox next to **User Defined 1**.

7. In the **Selected Fields** scrolling window, scroll down to the bottom and mark the **Account Number** field; this will make it available on the **Condition** tab in the field list without needing to marking the **Display extended field list**.

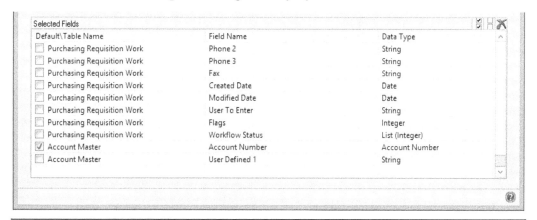

8. Click the **Link Tables** button on the toolbar.

9. Set the first table to **Purchase Requisition Line**.

10. Leave the join type set to **Left Join**, as purchase requisitions are not required to have an **Account** (an inner join would be used when linking on a mandatory field).

11. Set the second table to **Account Master**.

12. In **Field 1**, select the **Inventory Index** and, in **Field 2**, select the **Account Index** to set the relationship between the **Purchase Requisition Line** and **Account Master** tables.

13. The join between the two tables above is a simple one, but some joins you may add may require a composite key (i.e. two or more fields on each side). To add a second field to join on, with **Field 2** the active field, hit the *Tab* key to add a second line.

14. Click the **Add** button to insert the relationship to the list of **Table Links**.

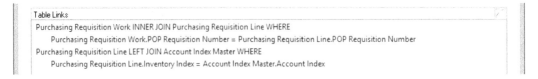

15. To verify that the relationship works, click the **Run Query** button on the tool bar.

16. Click the **Execute** button, to run the query. This will populate both the **T-SQL** section with the query and the **Results Preview** with the returned data.

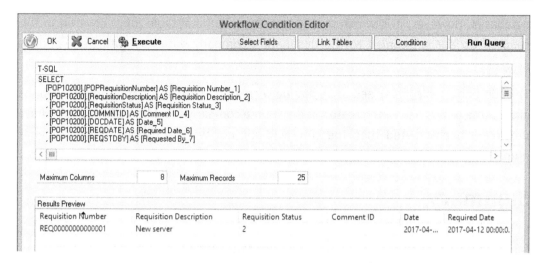

The T-SQL can be copied and used in SQL Server Management Studio to debug the generated SQL statement to ensure the table relationships are valid. If problems are found the relationship can be deleted, by selecting the **Table Link** in the **Link Tables** stage and clicking the cross button in the top right of the scrolling window.

17. The **Maximum Columns** and **Maximum Records** fields can be changed before clicking **Execute** to return more data for verification.

18. Once the relationships have been verified, the new fields are available for use in setting a condition. Click the **Conditions** button to change the view.

19. Mark the **Display extended field list** checkbox; this needs to be done otherwise fields from additional table relationships will not display in the list.

20. In the field drop down, select **Account Master.Account Number**.

21. Set the **Filter** to **contains**.

22. Enter *-1100-* in the **Value** field and click **Add**.

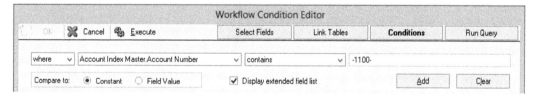

With the new relationship added, the remainder of the workflow process can be built as normal.

Copying a workflow with additional table joins

The Copy workflow function can be used to copy workflow processes between company databases. However, it is worth noting that the additional table joins, covered in this chapter, *do not get copied* to the destination company database with the workflow process.

The additional table joins need to be manually created in the destination company in the exact same order they were created in the source company. If additional table joins have previously been created then the copy will still not work correctly as the sequence numbers will be different.

Summary

In this chapter we have taken a look at how additional table relationships can be setup for a workflow type to allow the step conditions to be extended beyond the default fields. In the next chapter, we will take a look at the installation of the Web Services for Microsoft Dynamics GP which are required for workflow actions.

9

Installing Web Services for Microsoft Dynamics GP

Web Services for Dynamics GP is required if you intend to use the email actions component of Workflow 2.0. Email actions provide users the ability to review, approve and reject batches and transactions submitted for approval without the need to log into Microsoft Dynamics GP.

This chapter will cover the installation of the Web Services and their prerequisites and then the configuration and verification of the Web Services. After you have completed these steps you will be able to use the Email Actions.

Prerequisites

There are a number of prerequisites when installing the Web Services for Microsoft Dynamics GP.

First, the operating system; Windows Server 2008 R2, 2012, 2012 R2 Standard or Enterprise editions are supported.

Second, a Microsoft SQL Server 2012 or 2014 to host the security database. This could be the same or different SQL Server which is hosting the Microsoft Dynamics GP 2015 system and company databases.

Third, the Microsoft .NET Framework 4.5 is required and will be installed by the Microsoft Dynamics GP setup utility; I often find it best on servers to manually install this using the Windows Server Manager before starting the installation.

Fourth, a service user account is needed to run as the Microsoft Dynamics GP Service Host which is the Windows service host. If you're running Web Services on the SQL Server then you can use a local user account, but if the Web Services are on a different machine to the SQL Server then a Domain user account must be used.

Fifth, there are two bits of setup which need to have been completed in Microsoft Dynamics GP:

1. A **Functional Currency** needs to be configured in the **Multicurrency Setup** window (**Microsoft Dynamics GP menu >> Tools >> Setup >> Financial >> Multicurrency**)

2. All currencies need to have a unique **ISO** currency code (**Microsoft Dynamics GP menu >> Tools >> Setup >> System >> Currency**)

The remaining prerequisites are installed automatically when the setup.exe on the Microsoft Dynamics GP installation media is started. After starting the setup utility perform the following steps:

1. Click the **Install** button to begin the installation of prerequisites.

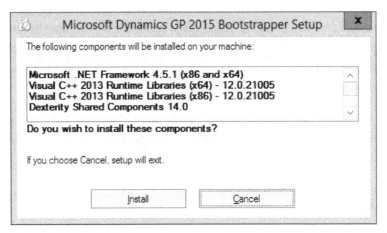

2. Once the installation of the prerequisites is complete, you may see the following dialog. Click **Yes** to reboot

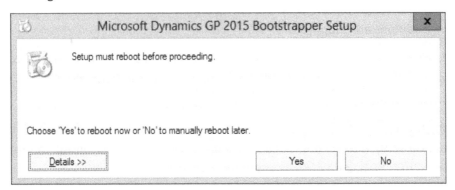

Not rebooting when prompted can cause issues with the installation of the Web Services, so I would always recommend rebooting before continuing, even if you are not prompted to do so.

Undocumented Prerequisite

One of the undocumented prerequisites for installing the Web Services, is that port 135 be closed on the firewall; technically this is not actually a prerequisite, but rather it is a bug known to Microsoft. However, I have been informed by Microsoft Support that it is one which is unlikely to ever be fixed due to it being a problem which only rarely occurs.

The bug means if the port is open on the firewall the configuration of Web Services will hang.

You do not need to stop and start the Configuration Wizard to resolve the issue; merely closing the port on the firewall will be sufficient to allow the configuration to proceed.

Installing the Web Services

Once you have the prerequisites installed you can move onto installing the Web Services themselves. To do this, perform the following steps:

1. Start the **setup.exe** on the installation media.

2. Under **Additional Products**, select **Web Services Runtime**.

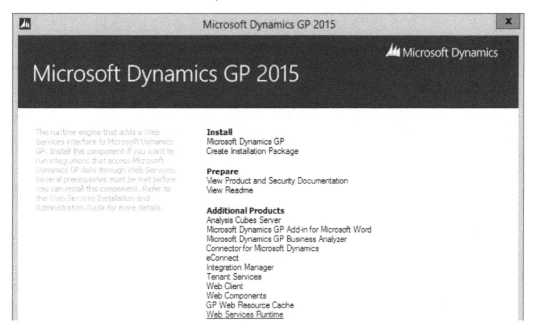

3. Mark the **I accept the terms in the License Agreement**.

4. Click **Next** to proceed to the next stage.

5. This is not a multi-tenant configuration so leave **Deploy for multiple tenants** unmarked and click **Next** to continue.

6. The details of the SQL Server holding the Microsoft Dynamics GP databases needs to be specified; in the **Server Name** field enter the SQL Server Name including the name of the Instance if a Named Instance of SQL is being used. I have entered `2016R1-SQL\GP` as I have a Named Instance called GP on the 2016R1-SQL server.

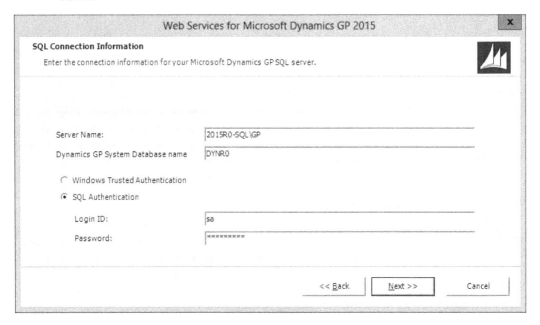

7. Enter the name of the **System Database** in the **Dynamics GP System Database** name field.

8. Choose an authentication method for connecting to the **SQL Server**; I typically use **SQL Authentication** to ensure the user using for the connection definitely has the correct permissions.

9. If you have chosen **SQL Authentication**, enter the **Login ID** and **Password** of a user which can access SQL Server; I usually use the **sa** account to ensure no permissions issues arise.

10. Click **Next** to continue.

11. Change the **Install Location** should you want to install somewhere other than the default location.

12. Click **Next** to continue.

13. Choose the location of the **Dynamics Security Data Store** which is where the security data will be stored.

    The recommended location is **SQL Server**; mark the relevant checkbox and click **Next** to continue.

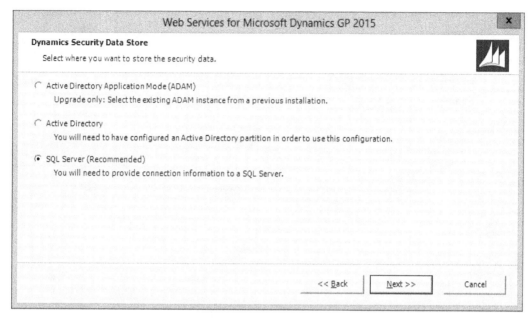

14. Now that SQL Server has been selected as the location of the **Dynamics Security Data Store**, the connection details of the **SQL Server** need to be entered.

    In the **Server Name** field enter the name of the SQL Server; this should include the name of the Instance if a Named Instance is being used.

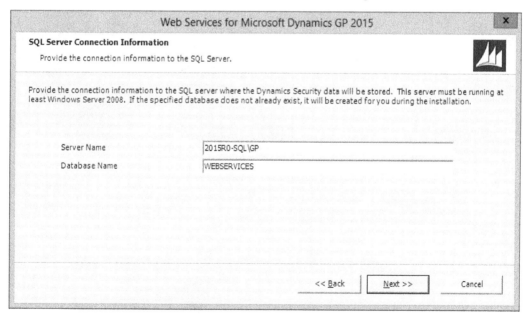

15. A default **Database Name** of WEBSERVICES will be displayed; this can be changed to something else should there be a requirement.

16. Click **Next** to continue.

17. It isn't possible here to specify the authentication method for this step, so you need to make sure the user you are logged into Windows with has permissions to create databases.

18. After clicking **Next** a check will be done to see if an existing security store exists on the specified SQL Server. If not a message confirming this will be displayed. Click **Next** to continue.

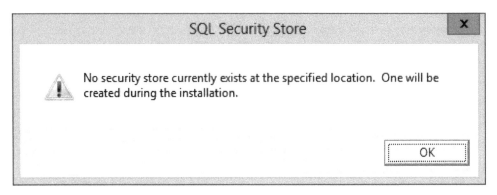

19. The **Application User Name** needs to be provided. This is the account which will be used as the service account.

When the Web Services are not being installed on the SQL Server a Domain account must be entered. This is the installation method I am using so I have entered the NETBIOS AZURECURVE and the Domain account user name and password.

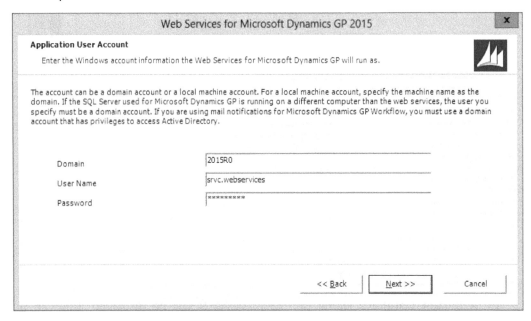

When using, as we are, Workflow email actions, the Domain user account must be one which has privileges to access Active Directory.

20. Click **Next** to continue.

21. The default ports for the Web Services will be displayed on the Service Ports step.

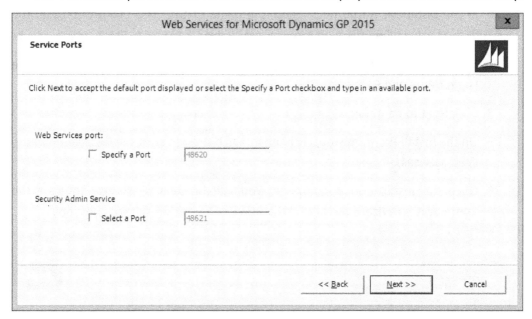

22. If different ports should be used, mark the relevant checkbox and enter a new port number.

23. Click **Next** when the ports are configured as required.

24. If you are using the Web Client, the **GP Workflow Service Configuration** step needs to be completed. To enable this step, mark the **Yes – Provide connection information to access configuration settings in the GP Configuration database**.

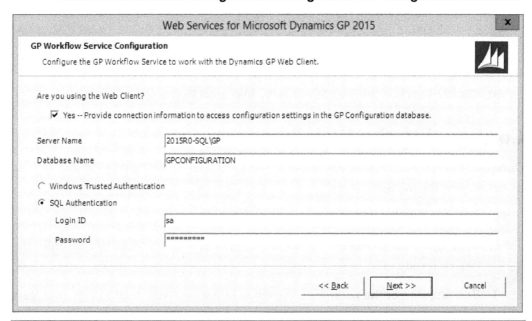

25. Enter the full name of the **SQL Server** including the **Instance Name**, if a named instance of SQL Server is being used, in the **Server Name** field.

26. In the **Database Name** field, enter the name of the Web Client database; the default value when the web client is installed is GPCONFIGURATION.

27. Select the authentication method and, if you chose **SQL Authentication**, enter the **Login Name** and **Password**.

28. Click **Next** to continue.

29. On the **Install Program** step, click the **Install** button to start the installation of the Web Services.

30. Once the installation is complete, you will be able to choose to start the **Configuration Wizard** by clicking the **Run Configuration Wizard** checkbox.

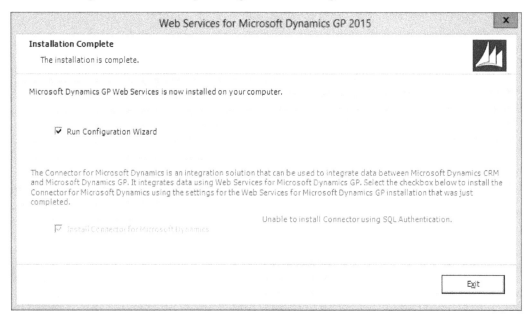

31. Click **Exit** to close the **Web Services for Microsoft Dynamics GP 2015 setup utility**.

Configuring the Web Services

Once the Web Services have been installed, they need to be configured for use. Do this by performing the following steps:

1. Click the **Windows Start** button.

2. Type gp web and select the **GP Web Services Configuration Wizard** from the search results.

3. The first step of the wizard is a **Welcome** one where you need to click the **Next**

button.

4. The **Connection Information** step has two fields, **SQL Server Name** and **SQL Server Log On Information**, which are set to the SQL Server Name, including the Instance name, configured during the installation, and **Windows Trust Authentication** which cannot be changed. Click **Next** to continue.

5. The **System Setup** check performs two checks; the first to make sure that all currencies have a valid **ISO** code and that all companies have a **Functional Currency** defined.

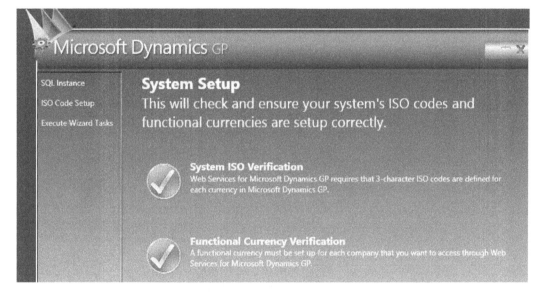

If the check does not return valid results for both, shown as white checks in green circles, you will need to correct the issue detected before continuing.

6. If both checks returned a valid result, click **Next** to continue.

7. The **Company Selection** window will display all of the companies in Microsoft Dynamics GP. Select all of the ones which should have the **Web Services** configured to use (the **Ctrl** and **Shift** keys can be used to select multiple companies).

8. Click **Next** to continue once all required companies have been selected.

9. The **Summary** step will list all of the selected companies. Check the list and make sure all of the ones you want to use **Web Services** with have been selected. Click **Next** to continue.

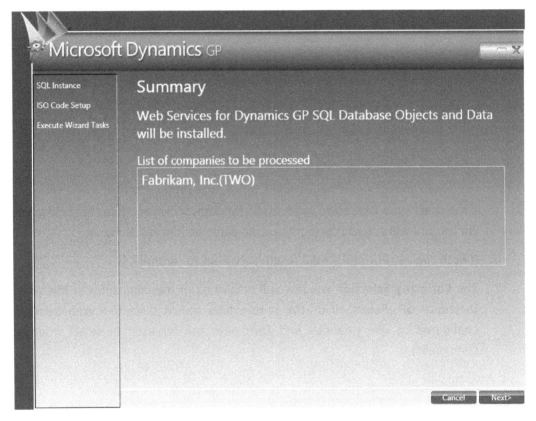

10. A dialog will be displayed asking for confirmation to continue with the install of **Web Services for Microsoft Dynamics GP**. Click **Yes** to proceed.

11. Once the install is complete a **Finished** step will be displayed. Click **Complete** to close the **GP Web Services Configuration Wizard**.

12. A final dialog will be displayed, asking if the Windows Service hosting the Web Services for Microsoft Dynamics GP should be restarted; click **Yes**.

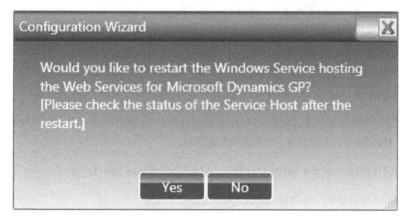

Verifying the Web Services

Once the configuration is complete, I would recommend verifying the Web Services to ensure everything is installed, configured and working correctly.

Windows Services

The first item to check is the Windows Services which host the Web Services and eConnect (which is installed automatically as the Web Services have a dependency on eConnect).

Do this by performing the following steps:

1. Open the **Services Control Panel** applet by clicking on the **Windows Start** button.

2. Type `services` and click on **Services**.

3. Instead of performing steps 1 and 2 you can press *Win+R*, type `services.msc`

and hit **Return**.

4. Scroll down the list and find **eConnect for Microsoft Dynamics GP 2015 Integration Service**; ensure it has **Running** in the **Status** column.

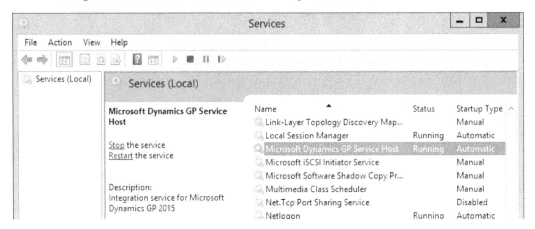

5. Scroll down and find the **Microsoft Dynamics GP Service Host** and ensure it has **Running** in the **Status** column.

6. Click the cross in the top right corner to close the **Services** window.

Web Services

The next step in the verification process, is to check that the Web Services themselves are running. To this by performing the following steps:

1. Launch **Internet Explorer** by clicking the **Windows Start** menu.

2. Type ie and click on Internet Explorer.

3. Alternatively, instead of performing steps 1 and 2, you can press *Win+R*, type `iexplore` and hit **Return**.

4. In the **Address Bar** enter `http://{server}:48620/DynamicsGP WebServices` (where {server} is the name of your server). If the Web Services are functioning correctly, you will see the following:

5. Next, in the **Address Bar** type `http://{server}:48620/Dynamics/` `GPService` (where {server} is the name of your server). If the web services are functioning correctly, you will see the following:

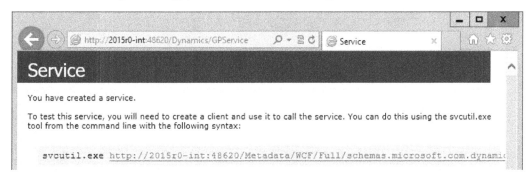

6. Click the cross in the top right corner to close **Internet Explorer**.

Security

The final step of the verification process is to verify the security. Do this by performing the following steps:

1. Click the **Windows Start** button.

2. Type `dynamics sec` and click on **Dynamics Security Console**.

3. Click **Yes** on the **User Account Control** prompt.

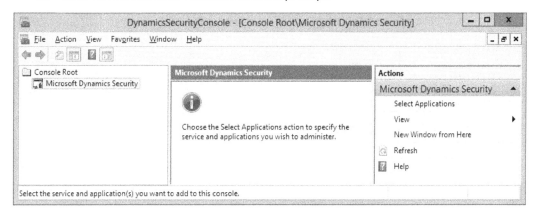

4. In the **Actions** pane, click on **Select Applications**.

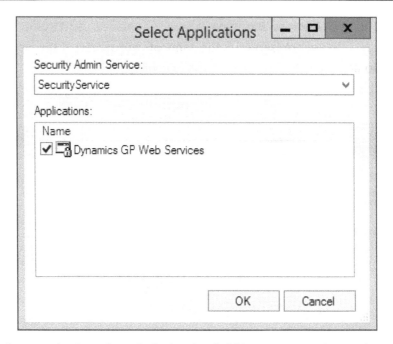

5. Make sure the **Security Admin Service** field is set to **SecurityService**.

6. Make sure the **Applications** list has **Dynamics GP Web Services** marked.

7. Click **OK** to accept the selection and close the **Select Applications** window.

8. Expand the **Microsoft Dynamics Security** Node.

9. Expand the **Microsoft Dynamics GP Web Services** node.

10. Click on **Policy**.

11. If you see the policies as shown above, the **Web Services** security has been correctly deployed. Click the cross in the top right corner to close the **DynamicsSecurityConsole**.

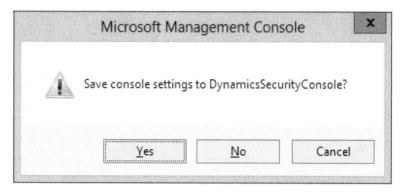

12. Click **Yes** on the **Save console settings** dialog.

Summary

In this chapter we have taken a look at how to install, configure and verify the Web Services for Microsoft Dynamics GP which are required if you want to use the Workflow 2.0 Email Actions.

Index

Thank you for buying

Microsoft Dynamics GP

Workflow 2.0

Second Edition

Visit http://publishing.azurecurve.co.uk **for other titles from azurecurve Publishing.**